Penguin Handbooks
Protect Your Property and Defend Yourself

Gordon Hasler was in the Army during the war
and for some years afterwards, when his training
in security matters ranged from the protection of
documents while on the staff, to 'unarmed combat'
as a parachutist. On leaving the Army he joined a
leading commercial security company, who
published his first book *Integrated Alarm Systems*.
Since the early 1970s he has been an independent
security consultant, operating in many parts of the
world and handling a wide range of assignments
from industrial espionage to computer security.
He is a Fellow of the British Institute of
Management, a Member of the British Computer
Society and Certified with the American Society
of Industrial Security. He lives in London and has
a grown-up family.

Gordon Hasler
Protect Your Property and Defend Yourself

Illustrated by Jo Whitley

Penguin Books

Penguin Books Ltd, Harmondsworth, Middlesex, England
Penguin Books Australia Ltd, Ringwood, Victoria, Australia
Penguin Books Canada Ltd, 2801 John Street, Markham, Ontario, Canada L3R 1B4
Penguin Books (N.Z.) Ltd, 182–190 Wairau Road, Auckland 10, New Zealand

Published in Penguin Books 1982

Made and printed in Great Britain by
Richard Clay (The Chaucer Press) Ltd, Bungay, Suffolk
Set in Monophoto Times

Contents

Foreword

One of the biggest problems, if not *the* biggest, besetting all developed nations throughout the world is crime. In 1980 the number of serious offences recorded by the police in England and Wales was 2,688,000, close to the previous peak of 1977. As in previous years, about 80 per cent of all the offences recorded were of theft and handling stolen goods (1,463,000) or of burglary (623,000). The figures for 1981 seem set to achieve even higher totals.

It is against this background that the role of the police as 'crime controllers' has to be examined. While over the past twenty years the strength of police forces has shown a steady if at times uncertain growth, the figures for recorded crime have increased at a considerably greater rate. It has become quite obvious that police alone cannot stem the tide – every member of the community has to play a part, and one of the most important aspects of this is that he should seek, as much as he can, to secure his own property against the criminal.

Mr Hasler's book, whilst not necessarily reflecting police policies in every respect, more particularly so far as intruder alarms are concerned, nevertheless contains a wealth of useful advice and will undoubtedly serve to inform those who are anxious properly to discharge their responsibilities in this important matter of the steps they can prudently take.

P.D.K.

by Sir Philip Knights, C.B.E., Q.P.M.,
Chief Constable, the West Midlands Police Force
which incorporates the Police Crime Prevention Centre

Acknowledgements

This book came about because of the ideas and enthusiasm of Cecil Abrahams. Not only did he conceive the original need for it, but he also helped with the research and read and criticized the manuscript as it went along. Above all he applied the encouragement and discipline to make it all happen.

Writing this book proved a more traumatic experience than I thought possible when I started out; my previous efforts were made so long ago that only the euphoria remained, but the patience and tolerance of my family, friends and business colleagues have made it all possible. My daughter Sarah somehow found time to type the manuscript while being the wife of a newly appointed curate in a very busy Manchester parish, where, in spite of her duties and priorities, she seemed to make the impossible both achievable and fun. Lance, my step-son, who has had experience in the security business, offered helpful and constructive comments, while an even more professional view was given to me by Ted Harris, Chief Securrity Officer of Tesco Stores (Holdings) Ltd, and Ray Forster, a District Commander of the London Fire Brigade.

Finally, my wife, Day, has as always been the main prop of my work; she has made the original idea actually happen, even resorting to taking me to Spain in the winter to get the work done. She has put up with all the moods and inconveniences that go with the writing process and still smiles deliciously at the end of it. I can never thank her enough.

Chapter 1
Security

1. Security

Our Changing Society

One of the more disturbing features of the rapid changes which have taken place in our society over the last decade has been the increase in crime. While statistics are available to demonstrate different aspects of the problem, the real effect is that nearly everyone knows that they are under threat of some kind of criminal attack – ranging from having their house burgled, their bicycle or car stolen, wallet or bag snatched, through to mugging and rape.

In this situation of threat you can either refuse to believe that it will ever happen to you or you can prepare yourself to face up to the problem. To really believe that you will never be a victim is clearly self-delusion, given all the stories told the moment the subject of theft or burglary is discussed with family, friends and neighbours. Almost certainly some of them will have been the target of a criminal attack in the last few years.

Taking a Balanced View

To take security to ridiculous lengths is just as unhealthy as doing nothing about it. In fact, achieving a reasonable and proper balance is probably the most difficult problem of all. This balance can only be achieved if a person faces up to the threats, understands what can be done to reduce the risks posed by those threats, and then takes steps to improve his security without unduly impairing his way of life.

Security, a State of Mind

Security is fundamentally a state of mind. In order to improve security people's attitudes need to be changed from complacent, frightened or just ignorant to confident, sensible and secure. Unfortunately, this is more easily said than done. People who are aware of being under threat may well pick on extreme solutions to their problem. It is not good security for a person who fears he may be robbed to carry a pistol or flick knife, nor for someone who feels he may be burgled to so bar up his house that it becomes a potential death-trap in the event of a fire.

In dealing with the problem of how to protect your property and defend yourself, I should therefore like to start by considering attitudes and how they may need to be changed. Attitude-change is achieved by getting people to:

a. Look at their situation;
b. Learn what it is possible to do to improve their position;
c. Decide on a course of action and carry it out;
d. Review their situation after taking action and from time to time in the future.

The process of considering security and doing something about it certainly costs time, possibly inconvenience and probably money. Furthermore, there must be some relationship between the value of the goods at risk and the measures taken to protect them. It would obviously be ridiculous to spend £2,000 on a good safe to hold jewellery worth no more than a few pounds – although this is better than an inadequate safe for jewels worth many thousands.

False Security

A person could well *feel* more secure because he had put valuable jewels in a safe of some kind, but though this is clearly preferable to leaving them in a drawer of the dressing table, there is a very real danger that the sense of security is being falsely achieved. When a determined thief gets into the house and easily opens that safe to remove the jewels, the owner will be shattered – not only because of the loss but also because his confidence in a safe has been destroyed. In fact, if there had been a proper quality safe for the value of the jewels concerned, the thief would almost certainly have been foiled.

Perfect Security

The 'almost certainly' in the last sentence above is a necessary qualification because there is no such thing as perfect security. People ask for their houses to be made 'burglar-proof', 'like Fort Knox' and so on, but such absolutes are impossible.

During the Great Exhibition of 1856, Chubb & Son were exhibiting a 'pick-proof' lock which a visiting American locksmith, Mr Hobbs, said he could open. The challenge was accepted and a wager laid, but Mr Hobbs insisted that the operation be carried out in public with full publicity. Of course, within an embarrassingly short time Mr Hobbs succeeded in picking the lock, thus winning the wager and making himself moderately famous. Chubb & Son learned the lesson well and never again described their wares as burglar-proof or fire-proof but rather thief-resistant or drill-resistant. Indeed, they were sufficiently successful to be able to buy up Mr Hobbs's company within a few years.

Security measures should therefore be designed to give a resistance to the attacks identified as threats to a degree that is acceptable to the person concerned. In some cases, teaching people to lock the front doors of their houses may be all that is required, while in others locks, bars, closed-circuit television and alarm systems may be necessary. Such 'hardware' plays an important role in maintaining security and will be discussed in detail, but it is by no means the whole solution. In many cases, security can be improved by the way people behave and present themselves. A young woman is obviously at risk if she habitually stays out late at night and returns along back streets to her flat. Her situation can be improved by changing her habits (of staying out late) or by taking a taxi home. Similarly, the victims of muggings are seldom healthy, apparently strong, young men – and while one can not change one's build, self-confidence and a determined bearing do put off prospective attackers.

Range of Subject

I have already mentioned attitudes, locks, safes, alarm systems, mugging, theft and fire. The range of topics is enormous and will be differently treated by everyone discussing the subject. In this book my aim has been to take a systematic approach so that readers can analyse their problems and obtain guidance in solving them. Just as there is no such thing as perfect security, there is no universal solution to all security problems: each is individual and can ultimately be solved only by the person concerned. The Appendices list police, fire services and security companies from whom further advice can be obtained.

A girl I know asked for advice because she had fallen out with her boyfriend and was afraid he might break into her flat. By putting some locks on the windows, a floodlight on the back patio and taking sensible precautions about returning there at night, she has felt relaxed about a situation which was previously ruining her health. At the other end of the spectrum, we were asked to recommend a system for ensuring that the drinking water for a Mid-Eastern ruler was continuously monitored. The solution in this case was to pass some of the water through a fish tank containing an electronic alarm system to give warning of the fish dying or becoming unusually active (if an additive had been put in the water). I found out later that in the past the same technique had been used by monks who only drank from the carp pond in their monastery.

Chapter 2
The Threats

2. The Threats

Statistics

Despite the old saying about 'lies, damned lies and statistics', some figures are important to illustrate the probability of certain occurrences. As the occupier of a house, flat or bedsitting room, you can be pretty sure that you will be robbed or burgled during your lifetime – at least once. The experience is extremely disturbing, and in some cases the sense of having privacy or possessions violated may even cause deep psychological damage. At the least, the losses are likely to be totally inadequately covered by insurance.

The statistics for this sort of crime are published every year by the Home Office and indicate that:

In 1977 there were	695,000 burglaries	and	18,000 robberies
,, 1978 ,, ,,	642,000 ,,	,,	17,000 ,,
,, 1979 ,, ,,	626,000 ,,	,,	16,000 ,,
,, 1980 ,, ,,	701,000 ,,	,,	19,000 ,,

These figures give the numbers of reported crimes but it is probable that at least twice this number again go unreported because people are often too frightened or upset to take any action or just will not have anything to do with the police. Over a fifty-year period of house occupancy, therefore, the total number of such crimes will be about 33,000,000 – or at least two per household. In fact, a burglary or robbery is taking place each minute of the day and night in Great Britain.

But figures alone do not mean a great deal to anyone – except statisticians and politicians. Far more convincing is the actual, first-hand experience of being the victim of such crimes. Haven't you, or your parents or some member of your family been burgled in the last year or so? Hasn't one of your neighbours been robbed in recent times? You probably also know someone who has been the victim of a more serious crime, like mugging, rape or assault.

'It won't happen to me'

It is very natural not to dwell on such matters otherwise life would become too threatening. The most common reaction is one of 'Poor them, but it

Figure 1. *What it means to be burgled*

won't happen to me.' Perhaps, but the odds are against you – unless you do something about it. The villains are real and multiply on the good living they make out of people's inaction.

The Villain

Touching on the figures again, in very simple terms it has been estimated that, of the total population, ten per cent are totally honest and incorruptible; eighty per cent will go along with the majority opinion; and ten per cent are dishonest and, short of an occasional miraculous conversion, will always remain so.

Neither Borstal, prison nor other corrective establishment is likely to alter the attitude of the out-and-out criminal. If his 'trade' is burglary he will have learned it well and will be a difficult person to guard against and defeat. But, because his time is precious, he will, like other offensive people, concentrate his attacks on the 'soft target' rather than the tough, well-defended one. In other words, a burglar will naturally choose a house which is easier to get into and out of than one which has obviously been given some measure of protection. Good descriptions of these villains are given in Peter Burden's book *The Burglary Business and You*.

The great mass of people – the eighty per cent in the figures given above – are not committed one way or the other. They will choose to act honestly if given firm direction – perhaps through upbringing or the circumstances in which they live and work – but could equally drift into dishonesty if

Figure 2. *Open windows are an open invitation – particularly if they are readily accessible*

temptations are put before them and it seems likely they will go undetected. Indeed, though the people in this group typically consider themselves law-abiding and respectable, the majority will cheat or steal in some way, perhaps without being properly conscious of it.

The responsibility of individuals not to subject others to temptation should therefore be far more widely recognized. In a case where some young people drive off a car without the owner's consent and then have a crash in which they sustain injuries, who is to blame? The young people's parents for not bringing them up properly? Their schoolteachers? The young people themselves? Perhaps – but if the car owner didn't bother to lock his car or maybe even to remove the ignition key it could be argued that he was by far the most culpable. He should not be eligible for any insurance cover and should perhaps even be prosecuted for being instrumental in causing injuries to the young people. This is in no way to condone the crime committed, but to point out that the responsibility for it should be more widely shared. Similarly, there should be little sympathy for house-holders who leave a window or back door open while they are out of the house (even for a short while) and come back to find their valuables stolen.

Spectrum of Crime

The more serious crimes against the person, such as assault, rape and kidnap, are discussed in detail in Chapter 5. Theft and related crimes are covered by the Theft Act of 1968, from which the following definitions are taken:

Theft: A person is guilty of theft if he dishonestly appropriates property belonging to another with the intention of permanently depriving the other of it. On conviction, a person shall be liable to imprisonment not exceeding ten years.

Robbery: A person is guilty of robbery if he steals and uses force, or the threat of force, on another person. The maximum penalty is imprisonment for life.

Burglary: A person is guilty of burglary if, in order to steal, he enters a building as a trespasser. The maximum penalty is fourteen years. If, however, aggravated burglary is committed (i.e. with the use of offensive weapons, such as fire-arms or explosives) the maximum penalty again becomes life imprisonment.

Fraud: A person is guilty of fraud who, by deception, dishonestly obtains property belonging to another. The maximum penalty is ten years.

Incidentally, stealing and thieving are the same thing.

Once goods have been stolen, they have to be disposed of. This usually means using receivers. Receivers work in one of two ways – they either:

a. Specialize in certain items and instruct their own team of thieves to obtain specific items (e.g. porcelain figures) from a house where it is known these items are owned, at a time when there is a buyer for the goods; or

b. Buy the items they may be interested in from thieves who have worked for themselves.

In either case, the receiver will seldom pay more than a tenth of the value he will expect to receive for the items. This of course explains why cash is particularly attractive to a thief of any kind – in addition, it is almost impossible to identify (for who makes a note of the serial numbers on their money?).

The receivers try to sell off their stolen goods through well-established and, they hope, well-covered channels or outlets. If you've been burgled it's often well worth checking street markets in or around your town, because current legislation makes them a safer outlet than shops. If a shop tries to sell goods which are subsequently identified as having been stolen, those goods have to be surrendered and the shop loses them. If, however, the goods are on sale at a legitimate street market, they are not automatically surrendered. Undoubtedly, the police would wish to make searching inquiries of the stallholder into where and from whom he obtained the goods, but if his answers prove satisfactory, the owner has to pay the stallholder to repossess his goods.

How, though, would you identify your goods? Of course you think you know your own camera, silver, TV, tape recorder, bicycle, jewellery, watch or whatever. But you can only properly establish ownership by being able to produce a photograph of them or by knowing their serial numbers. It really doesn't take long to have a good check around the house and make a list of all the equipment with serial numbers – from the washing machine to your watches. You will probably end up with a surprisingly long list, but once made it will be easy to keep up to date. Get a photocopy and leave it in a sealed envelope with a close relative or your bank. Photographs of jewellery, pictures, porcelain and silver can be kept in the same sealed envelope. The best way to photograph valuables is to place a piece of dark material on the floor, set out a suitable collection of items and take a colour flash photo of them. Change the items and do it again. It is well worth using half a reel of film – and you don't need to give your address to the photographer who develops them. If the items are of considerable value, it is worth while obtaining the services of a professional Fine Art and Antique Photographer. However, be careful to check the photographer's credentials before exposing your goods to his camera.

Unfortunately it has to be said that the chances of recovering stolen goods are fairly slight. But those chances will be immeasurably improved if the goods can be identified with photographs or serial numbers.

At certain times particular crimes seem to become more prevalent – such as a wave of muggings over some months – and then fade in 'popularity'. The reasons for this phenomenon are usually a combination of:

- Police success at dealing with the particular crime by a special effort in that direction;
- The public realizing the danger or threat to themselves individually because of the publicity and taking sensible steps to reduce their risks;
- The criminals or prospective criminals finding that this particular activity has suddenly become more difficult/dangerous than another way of thieving or robbing.

Over the years, however, crimes of violence are totally consistent in their continual steady rise, and though the numbers of burglaries and thefts may fluctuate, criminals continue to use them as a steady reliable living.

Check List

1. What sort of person is most likely to be a threat to you?
2. At what times would a burglar find it easiest to get into your house? During the day, the weekend, when you are on holiday?
3. In what circumstances? When you go out to lunch, to the theatre, or just round the corner to the shops?
4. How is he likely to try to get in? Through the back door, an open window, the cat flap, or a trick to make you think he is a meter reader?
5. If you were locked out of your house, how would *you* get in without rousing the neighbours? If you could, a thief would certainly be able to do the same.
6. What are you likely to have stolen? TV, camera, clock, watches, cash left around, hi-fi, typewriter, glass, china, silver, jewellery, furs, pictures, furniture etc.?
7. Have you made a list of serial numbers of those goods which have them and taken photographs of all other special items in 6 above?
8. Are you fully insured?
9. Do you know how to call the police in an emergency and do you know who your local Crime Prevention Officer is?

Chapter 3
Physical Defences

3. Physical Defences

The Maginot Line

Before World War II the French built up a sophisticated and very impressive defence system against their expected enemy. The system consisted of hugely powerful fortresses cut into the hills of east and north-east France, with connecting tunnels to allow supplies and reinforcements to be moved safely from one to the other. There were huge stocks of food and water, an electricity generating system, and plenty of ammunition for the defending guns, whose barrels protruded from the armoured casements.

The French were rightly proud of their engineering achievement and confident in a system which had cost them many millions of francs, so when war was about to be declared in 1939 they removed the preserving grease from their weapons. However, when the Germans attacked in May 1940, they used gliders and parachutists on certain of the forts, capturing them and breaching the Line in less than forty-eight hours.

The lesson to be learned was that physical defences need to be kept up to date with developing techniques of attack. A relatively small defence effort on top of the forts, or in trenches in front of them, could easily have repelled the German attacks. Thus any defence system must be considered from the point of view of the likely attack or threat of attack. Equally, the defence system must always be complete, in the sense that there should be no way around, over, under or through the barriers of the 'fortress' or strong point.

This may seem a long way from your home, whether it be a mansion or 'pad', but the basic principles are the same. Imagine that what you are defending (e.g. jewellery or furs) is placed at the centre of a number of concentric rings of defence (see Figure 3). These consist of the perimeter (e.g. garden wall), skin of building (e.g. house), room walls (e.g. bedroom), and container (e.g. safe or cupboard). Looked at in this way it may seem difficult for a prospective attacker to get at his 'target' in the centre. But this will only be the case if the whole system is coordinated and there are no obvious weaknesses or gaps in the defence rings. Let us therefore consider each of these rings or barriers in turn.

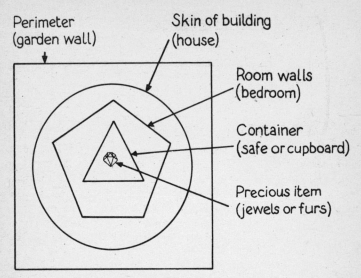

Figure 3. *Your home: concentric rings of defence*

Perimeter

If you live in a flat this section may not appear to concern you; but the perimeter in this case will be the outside walls of the building in which you live. Whatever the perimeter consists of, it should provide a means of delaying or, better still, dissuading a possible intruder and guiding him to a controlled entry-point where he may be identified.

On the continent many gardens are surrounded by high walls or iron railings, with entrance restricted to a remotely controlled locked gate. In this case, as with the front door to a block of flats, there is usually a communication system which allows a visitor to ring a bell, announce himself, and then be admitted through the perimeter barrier. Such a system often consists of a telephone handset in the house or flat and a loudspeaker/microphone by the front door or gate (Figure 4). Once the caller has identified himself the door can be electrically released. Flat-dwellers should remember that it is extremely irresponsible and unfair to their neighbours to allow someone into the block to visit another flat, unless this has previously been arranged.

Closed-circuit television can be used for more positive identification than voice alone, and this, together with other means of surveillance and access control, will be discussed in Chapter 6. Other devices can give warning

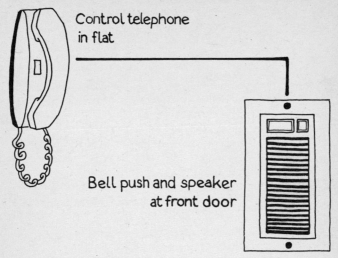

Control telephone
in flat

Bell push and speaker
at front door

Figure 4. *Phone to control energy*

that someone has gone through the gate or openings in the perimeter, such as a bell when the gate is opened, a noise mechanism when it closes, or even sophisticated detecting devices (see Chapter 4, Detectors).

Figure 5. *Section through ha-ha*

At the same time, it is important that possible intruders should be dissuaded from crossing the perimeter at any point other than the entrance gate. This can, of course, be achieved by a number of means, including:

- Walls around the property of reasonable height, at least 7 feet (2 metres) if possible, without any trees overhanging them to give an easy way over;
- Fences, made up of anything from chain-link or weldmesh to wooden or concrete palisades;
- Hedges, which should be as thick and high as possible and preferably of an 'antisocial' type such as holly or thorn. These can be improved as barriers by the inclusion of wire fencing through their bases.

In the past the owners of large country houses often used a 'ha ha', a form of ditch, as a boundary for their grounds so that they could enjoy an uninterrupted view (Figure 5).

Barbed wire and even razor wire can be used for fences (Figure 6), but it is inadvisable to use dangerous materials such as broken glass on top of walls. This is because everyone has a responsibility not to contribute to another citizen harming himself. For the same reason, man traps should

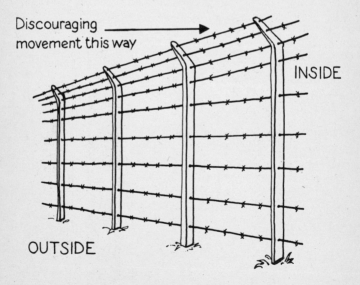

Figure 6. *Perimeter fencing with barbed wire*

not be used in houses: if an intruder was killed by one the owner would be liable to a charge of manslaughter.

Skin of Building

This is the house itself – or the front door and walls of the flat – forming a shell, generally consisting of walls, door(s), windows and a roof. The object of this shell is to exclude everyone from the house or flat except those you positively identify and allow in.

The ways through the shell are usually by means of the doors, windows and possibly the roof skylight, so these are the areas which require the greatest attention. However, bear in mind that the structure of some buildings is such that an intruder may be able to get through thin plaster walls or a light tiled roof more easily than through a stout front door!

Doors. Whether front, back or side doors, all should be equally strong. Kick them, put your weight against them, bang on them hard with your

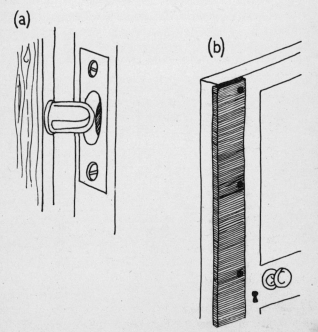

Figure 7. *Doors: (a) Hinge (reinforcing) bolt (b) Leading edge of door strengthened*

fists and you will soon establish whether or not they are substantial. If not, particularly if they have glass or panels in them, they should be strengthened or replaced. This can be done with metal bars, expanded metal (a steel mesh) or steel sheet fixed to the inside of the door. Check also that the door frame and its fixings to the wall are sufficiently strong – burglars do remove the whole door with its frame if that is the simplest means of entry.

Next, the doors should be well fixed and fastened with locks. The hinges must be substantial and not easy to get at because they can be taken apart if they are exposed. The hinge side can be strengthened with hinge bolts which can be fixed to the door to prevent it being forced in (Figure 7a). The leading edge (where the lock is) of the door can also be strengthened if necessary to prevent interference with the lock. An example of the flat steel edging used is shown in Figure 7b, but it should be pointed out that determined burglars sometimes use this metal edging as a levering surface when they try to force the lock with a crowbar or similar tool.

There is a bewildering selection of locks which can be used on these outside doors. The basic rules are that the locks should be mortice deadlocks (preferably of the 5-lever type), and that they should conform to British Standard 3621. Examples are shown in Figure 8. But remember that *all* the outside doors should be equally strong and have similar types of lock – the intruder will always seek out the weakest point. With the key anyone can open the door; do *not* leave it near the house (under a flower pot or on a string) or attach your address to it.

I knew a security salesman who sold a quantity of expensive locks to a breeder of silver foxes who had been losing valuable animals from his kennels. Shortly afterwards the angry customer rang to say that he had again been robbed in spite of the locks and it was found that this time the leather hinges of the kennel doors had been cut with a razor. The lock salesman had in fact done a particularly poor security job by selling only a part of the solution to the problem, and moreover probably aggravated it by disturbing the customer's confidence in locks.

It should always be remembered that outside doors are for the proper use of the people in the house (or flat). As such, the occupants must be able to get out whenever they need to and must not be so locked and bolted in that they cannot escape, for instance, in case of an outbreak of fire (see Chapter 7). This same consideration will apply in the section on windows and skylights below (see Figure 9a).

Windows and skylights. These are usually the weakest points in the shell. The problem lies in making them reasonably secure while still allowing them to be used for their proper purposes of providing light, a view and

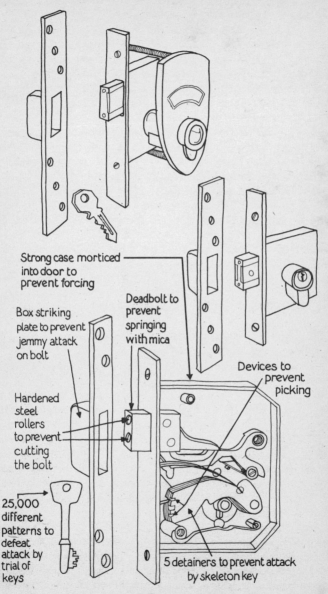

Strong case morticed into door to prevent forcing

Box striking plate to prevent jemmy attack on bolt

Deadbolt to prevent springing with mica

Hardened steel rollers to prevent cutting the bolt

Devices to prevent picking

25,000 different patterns to defeat attack by trial of keys

5 detainers to prevent attack by skeleton key

Figure 8. *Types of suitable security locks for front and back doors*

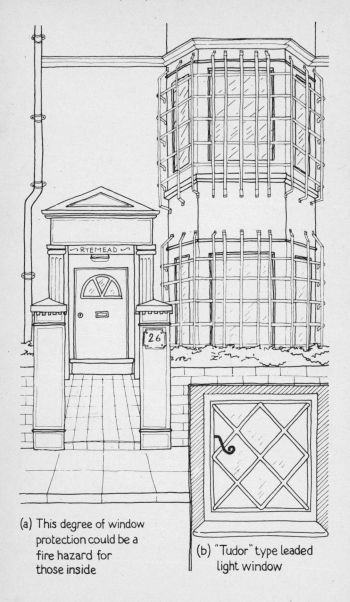

(a) This degree of window protection could be a fire hazard for those inside

(b) "Tudor" type leaded light window

Figure 9. *Window security*

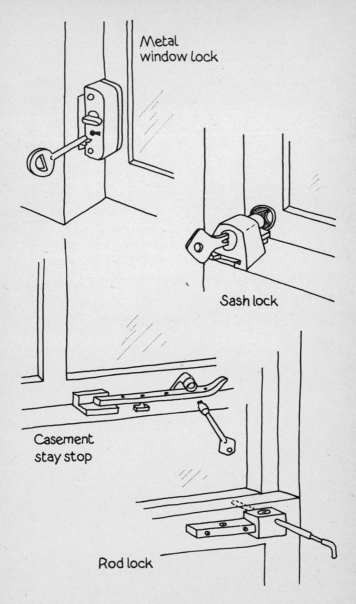

Metal
window lock

Sash lock

Casement
stay stop

Rod lock

Figure 10. *Window locks*

fresh air. As with outside doors, the windows and their frames should be sound. If they are not strong in themselves they should be strengthened. The most obviously weak windows in this context are leaded lights, where it is possible to push in the glass with very little pressure against the decorative panes (Figure 9b).

Where windows need strengthening a number of steps can be taken such as:
- Double glazing;
- Fixing security film (made of polycarbonate plastic) to the inside of the glass and attaching it firmly to the window;
- Installing polycarbonate glass or a similar non-shatter material in addition to or instead of the panes.

Once again the strength and fixings of the window frames themselves need looking at carefully to ensure they are as strong as the improved windows.

A window lock of some kind is needed in all cases where the window can be got at from the outside of the building. The catches which are installed by window suppliers are – almost without exception – designed to make it easy to open and close the window rather than genuine security devices to prevent an intruder opening it from outside. Examples of suitable locks are shown in Figure 10.

Bearing in mind that a burglar can usually get hold of a ladder or climb a drainpipe, look at your building from the outside and see whether there are *any* windows which should not be strengthened and locked.

The problems posed by french windows and patio doors are particularly acute, not only because they usually lead straight out on to a garden or balcony but because their very size makes them difficult to protect. In the past a lock known as an espagnolette was used (Figure 11a). Although this secured the doors well, it only required a hole to be made in the glass near the handle to make it possible to get at the lock. With the modern type of sliding panels the situation is even worse as these panels can normally be levered upwards and removed bodily from the channels in which they slide. All such windows should have special steel locks installed which will prevent them being opened and will also bolt them to the rails. (Figure 11b).

Another very common method of protecting window openings is to use bars or grilles. These can range from steel rods firmly embedded in the structure of the walls, not more than 5 inches (13 cm) apart, to decorative ironwork and moveable grilles which can be raised and lowered or moved from side to side, like lift gates (Figure 12). These all need to be professionally fitted. Again, the danger of making a fire trap must be appreciated when bars or grilles are installed.

Skylights or roof lights pose a different kind of problem. They may well

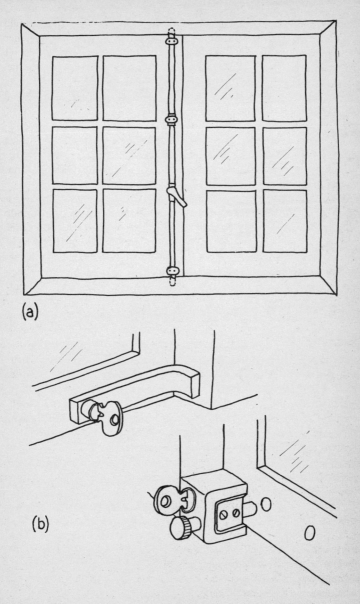

Figure 11. (a) *French window with espagnolette bolt* (b) *Locks for sliding doors*

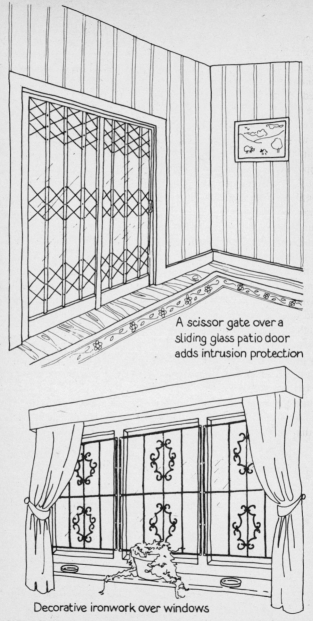

A scissor gate over a
sliding glass patio door
adds intrusion protection

Decorative ironwork over windows

Figure 12. *Window bars and grilles*

not need to be opened except in an emergency, but since they are usually far from the occupier's scrutiny they may be worked on by a burglar without being seen. Double glazing or polycarbonate glass on the skylight, associated with sound frames and good strong locks, should achieve the desired result.

The ability of burglars to climb up the outside of buildings is remarkable. They can be discouraged from making use of drainpipes by painting the pipes with 'anti-climb paint'. This paint has the quality of never hardening, so that it forms a slippery, jelly-like surface which is difficult for a climber to grip onto. It should not, however, be used on the pipes below a level of about 9 feet ($2\frac{1}{2}$ metres) so that innocent people do not rub against it.

Ventilators, air-conditioning inlets and cat or dog flaps are other ways through the skin of a building. Each of these has at some time been used by burglars. Such entries should be kept as small as possible, but if they become more than 12 inches (30 cm) across any of their measurements steps should be taken to prevent an intruder getting through. This can be done by firmly screwing equipment (such as an extractor) on the inside, by putting additional bars across the inside or by using a grille of some kind to cover the opening. Another point to remember is that cat or dog flaps should not be sited in such a way that a burglar could easily put an arm through to unbolt the door.

Basements or lower-ground-floor areas are particularly vulnerable, generally providing an intruder with somewhere he can hide while he works at overcoming the physical defences. Because of this many houses already have bars on the windows at this level, but often doors and locks are not adequately strengthened. It cannot be emphasized too often that the villain will always be looking for the weak link in the chain of defence so make sure that *all* doors and windows are equally strong.

Room Walls

The next stage of the rings of defence are the sides of the rooms themselves. These are really just partitions of the living space and as such they are probably better used as a trap for the burglar than a physical barrier. If you firmly lock all the internal doors of the house or flat it may cause an intruder some inconvenience. But remember that once inside he has the time and cover to break down doors with comparative ease – and the cost of repairing the damage may be greater than the value of goods stolen.

The best plan is to keep internal doors shut but not locked, and rely on the fact that, for the intruder, going into each room will be taking a step into the unknown – where new dangers may lie. The next chapter discusses how these doors and internal areas can be used as part of a trap in conjunction with alarms. For this reason it is important that the doors fit properly and that the latches or catches on them hold the doors shut when they are closed.

Containers

The holder in which you place your precious objects will, of course, depend upon what you are protecting – the smaller the object the more solid the container can be. Money, jewellery, silver and gold are best kept in a safe of some kind. Fur coats, large ornaments and bulky items of precious metals should have some form of strong, protected cupboard, while documents should be kept in a filing cabinet, preferably of the fire-resistant type.

Safes come in all shapes and sizes ranging from wall safes, through various under-floor types to the large free-standing variety (Figure 13). Their cost will depend upon their size and quality, but this is one area not to be mean about: if you are going to have a safe, get a decent one. Wall safes are usually made of steel and rely on the fact that they are concealed and that their sides and back cannot be got at except by removing the brick wall. However, once discovered, they can be relatively easily broken into. (It should go without saying that owners of safes should not broadcast the fact, still less mention how they have been hidden.)

The under-floor safe should be sunk in a hole in the floor, which is then filled with concrete. The manufacturer of the safe concentrates its strength in the upper surface and cover; this last is sometimes screwed on for strength before it is locked. Again, the walls of this safe are difficult to get at – because of the concrete – and if its top is well concealed (by a carpet or furniture) as well as strong, a good level of security will be achieved.

The larger, free-standing safes rely on their inherent strength to resist attack. What is more, if they weigh less than half a hundredweight (25 kg) they must be securely bolted to the floor by the manufacturer (or his agent) to prevent them being carried off bodily. The materials used in the better makes of modern safes are very sophisticated and are designed and tested to resist all kinds of attacks from drilling, burning by blowtorch, to picking of the lock or explosive attack (this last will usually deadlock the modern safe). Safes of this category are all numbered and named by their manufacturers, who will be only too glad to tell you which safe is appropriate for the value of items you will keep in it. Alternatively, your insurance company should also be able to advise you on the 'rating' of the safe you should buy.

Large old houses often had a Silver Room, which was most often situated under the lower stairs in the basement. This was usually a strongly built

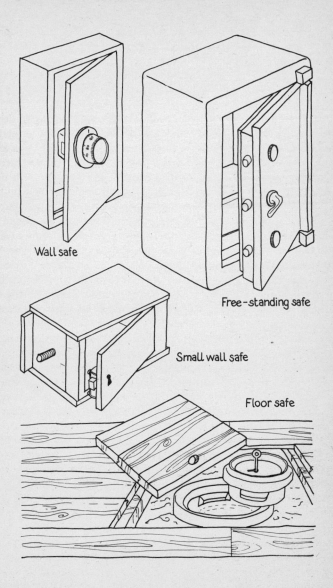

Wall safe

Free-standing safe

Small wall safe

Floor safe

Figure 13. *Safes*

windowless room, entered by a steel door with high quality locks. Such a room was good security in its day – and even nowadays it is a great deal better than most people have. Its disadvantage is that it concentrates the attractions in one place from which the determined thief will not have a great deal of difficulty extracting them (either by forcing the door or breaching the brickwork). If you are lucky enough to have such a room then either strengthen the walls and replace the door with a small strong-room one, i.e. a steel door with mechanical locking bolts, or have the room well covered with an alarm.

The same general principles will apply to whatever container you decide to store your valuables in. Whether you put them in a jewel case or biscuit tin the thief is sure to find them eventually, unless you are unusually clever in the way in which you hide them. Intending thieves often gather information by masquerading as meter readers, antique dealers, cleaners or even decorators, so always be vigilant when you allow a stranger into your home.

It would obviously be desirable if, in addition to physical defences, someone could be at home most of the time. If this is impossible, then irregular visits by a number of people at various times is very helpful – there is nothing a would-be burglar likes better than a house which operates to accurate schedules, with no one in it every day from, say, 9.30 to 11 in the morning and 3.30 to 4.30 every afternoon (school delivery/shopping/collecting). Leaving milk on the doorstep and newspapers hanging out of the letter box all day are also invitations to villains, who can double check that no one is in by ringing the front-door bell. When you are out for the evening or away on holiday, having your lights operated by a time switch can act as a deterrent.

So make sure your defences are complete – all windows and doors, however small or remote, being equally well covered. Don't forget the possibility of someone getting in through the roof or by removing an air vent or going up a fire escape. If you choose to hide valuables, remember that the thief knows all the usual tricks of concealment, like the hems of curtains, tops of pelmets, talc tins etc. And if you decide on a safe of some kind, make sure it's of the appropriate rating for what you intend to keep in it.

Check List

1. Is there a perimeter around your home and does it have a controlled entry-point?

2. How could you get into your house if you got locked out by mistake?
3. Are the back and front doors equally strong?
4. Have those doors, and any other entrance doors, got strong mortice deadlocks?
5. How physically strong are the windows, particularly at ground level, and have they got proper locks on them?
6. Have you got double glazing or bars on the windows or strengthened glass at basement level?
7. Is the front or back door masked by a porch and have you therefore made the door and its lock particularly strong?
8. Are the outside door frames strong and well fixed into the wall? Try pushing hard against the door when it is locked.
9. How easy is it to get on to the roof or in to the basement and can someone there be seen be passers-by?
10. Do you really check on strangers who call on you – before letting them into your house? Will you show your possessions to 'dealers' and do you always ask meter readers for their identity cards? If they do not have one would you report them and not let them in?

Chapter 4
Alarm Systems

4. Alarm Systems

Juno's Geese

We have seen how to achieve a measure of protection by physical means. We can strengthen our surrounds so that they will be extremely difficult for the prospective intruder to break through. In fact, we hope that because he recognizes the difficulty, he will decide to go elsewhere to do his burglary. However, it is also quite clear that a determined attacker can overcome physical defences. There is no such thing as a thief-proof safe or pick-proof lock – good safes and locks are thief-resistant. That resistance will delay the attacker for a given period of time which should be used to alert someone to respond to the attack and, hopefully, to stop it. The way to achieve this is to use an alarm system.

There is of course nothing new about using alarms. When the Gauls were attacking Rome in about 390 BC, their commander appreciated that the key to the city was the Capitol, the capture of which would demoralize the Romans. The Capitol was on a steep hill at the top of which were kept a flock of geese near a temple dedicated to the goddess Juno. The Gauls mounted a night attack on Capitol Hill but, in spite of a very quiet approach, they were heard by Juno's geese, which immediately let out a loud squawking. This aroused the defenders, who turned out and beat off the intruders.

The use of animals is a practical means of having a form of alarm, and it could be helpful to keep a large, fierce-looking dog on your property. However, a number of considerations should be taken into account. Dogs are often affected by the nervousness of their owners and may start barking for many reasons other than at intruders. Also they can be – and regularly are – very rapidly silenced by burglars who have absolutely no qualms about poisoning them or kicking their teeth in. Dogs are of value as an aid to security if they are properly trained and used for a specific task, but a pet which is loved and encouraged to be friendly to visitors is unlikely to be very effective as a guard dog – nor is he meant to be: as such he can be a considerable responsibility.

Juno's geese were properly used as an alarm system in the case quoted. They are birds with a particularly acute sense of hearing, so they detected

the approach of the Gauls. Their brains decided that this night-time movement was caused by intruders and that something should be done about it.
Accordingly they created such a commotion that the Roman soldiers were
roused from their sleep and beat off the attack. The geese demonstrate the
three parts of an alarm system:

   a. Detectors – the ears of the geese;
   b. Controls – their brains for evaluating the information and triggering
      off the signal;
   c. Signalling – the squawking which roused the defenders (the Re-
      sponse).

In any alarm system each of these parts must be capable of carrying out
its function fully at all times when needed. The detectors must be able to
recognize any real intruder and should not be deceived, either by operating
when there is no intruder or by not operating when there is one. The
controls should be easy to use and be capable of making the system live
when required, as well as being able to differentiate between an accidental
operation by a detector and a real emergency. The controls must also be
able to set off whatever signal or signals may be needed: often more than
one method of signalling may be involved. Finally, the signal itself must
operate effectively and alert the defenders.

Electric Alarms

The most practical and widely used alarms are electrically operated. These
have been in existence for about a century, so one would expect them to
have reached a high degree of reliability and sophistication: the fact that in
many cases they appear to fall short of this standard is often due to a lack
of knowledge in those using them.

The electric current used for alarms is of low voltage, because this is
easier and safer to handle and makes it possible to run them off batteries
if necessary. The great majority of intruder alarms now use 12 volts, as do
the majority of motorcars. A few smaller systems still use 6 volts (as do
most motorcycles), while fire-alarm systems are often on 24 or 48 volts.
Let us, however, stay with the generally used 12-volt system and go on to
see how it actually works.

When a light goes on in the room of a house it is usually an indication
that someone has gone into that room. In the alarm context, the switch
has acted as the detector, the power supply as the controls and the light as
the signal (Figure 14a). There are many systems which operate in such a

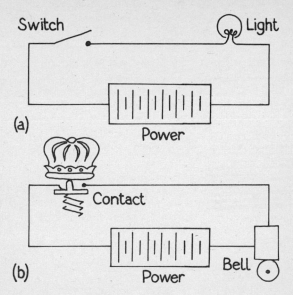

Figure 14. *Electric alarm systems*

simple way – for instance, refrigerator doors operate a switch, called a contact, which turns on the light when the door is opened.

If a contact from a refrigerator were installed under a valuable object and connected through a power source (such as a battery) to a bell, as in Figure 14b, you would have an alarm system. Should the valuable object be removed from the contact, the switch would operate and power would make the bell ring. The drawbacks of such a system are that it can easily be deceived by substituting another object for the valuable one and that it can only be tested by actually removing the object from the contact.

The solution is to arrange the circuits and controls into a closed-circuit system, which can be tested at any time and which will include protection against the circuit itself being tampered with or cut. In this way, any breaking of the current will cause the alarm system to operate. This, then, is the simplest form of detector.

Detectors

When the system is switched on, therefore, any cutting of the circuit wiring will cause an alarm condition and activate the signal. The wiring can then be formed into a barrier as shown in Figure 15a. An attacker attempting to get through the barrier would have to cut the wire; if he tried to move it aside it would in any case (if properly tensioned) snap. This type of wiring has many applications – on walls, ceilings or (sometimes) floors it acts as a barrier which can be covered over with normal room decorations. It can be used across windows, either within metal tubes or stuck on the glass as metal foil (Figure 15b and c). It is particularly effective when fixed on wooden surfaces such as doors or the sides and top of a box surrounding a safe. In all these cases the quality of the workmanship is most important and as a detector this wiring is cheap in the materials used but expensive in labour costs.

Pressure Pads. A different form of wiring is used with pressure pads. This detector device is usually a thin envelope of plastic, containing two layers of metal foil, separated by a sheet of foam with a number of holes in it. When this pad is placed on the floor, beneath the carpet (but above the underlay) where it cannot be seen, the weight of a person treading on it will press the upper metal foil against the lower one, squeezing the foam material, and so make metal to metal contact through one of the holes. This will act as a switch for the system because the metal strips will be part of the alarm.

Such a device is useful when concealed under carpets near windows through which an intruder may come, or in the corridor or on the stairs up which he may pass. Care has to be taken to ensure that furniture is not left on pressure pads and, of course, having animals in the house who may jump on them will cause endless trouble.

Mechanical Contacts. The mechanical contact is one which relies upon a direct physical operation of the mechanism, as with a refrigerator's light switch or the courtesy light switch on a car. Such contacts are generally used only where the movements of mechanical surfaces need to be detected, such as inside a lock or the lid of a metal box. However, they do have limitations, particularly in damp conditions or where they can be interfered with.

Magnetic Contacts. The magnetic contact is one that is operated by the influence of a magnet brought into close proximity to it. The contact itself (the switch) consists of two flat, overlapping strips of metal, in a small sealed glass tube. The flat strips are polarized so that the overlapping strips are of opposite poles, and when the magnet is brought close to them the ends are pushed towards each other and make electrical contact. When the magnet is removed the contacts spring apart (Figure 16).

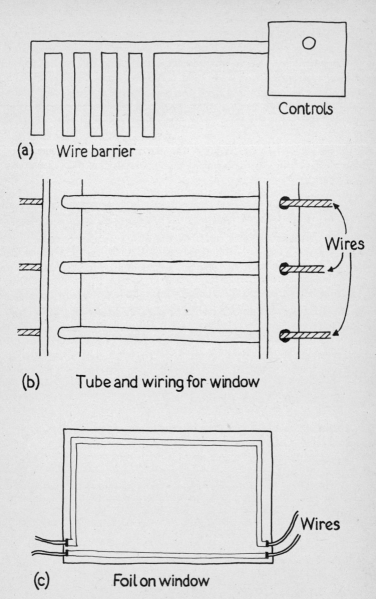

(a)   Wire barrier

(b)   Tube and wiring for window

Wires

(c)   Foil on window

Wires

Figure 15. *Types of barrier detector*

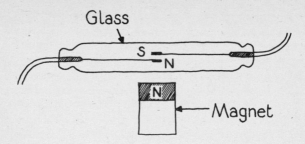

Figure 16. *Magnetic contact*

In this contact there is no frictional movement and it can be operated many millions of times without trouble. The glass tube, with the contacts, may be only ½ inch (12 mm) long and is usually encapsulated in a plastic holder. This half of the contact is installed on the fixed part of the structure, i.e. in the door or window frame, well away from the hinge. The magnet is fitted into the door itself or the moving part of the window, opposite the contact when the door or window is closed. Again, the current of the alarm system is passed through the leaves of the contact which are kept together by the magnet when the door or window is kept closed. Opening either will remove the magnet, causing the strips to spring apart and break the current, so activating an alarm.

Infra-red Rays. Invisible rays are widely used to detect the movement of people past such places as the automatic ticket barriers at the entrance to

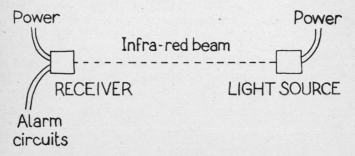

Figure 17. *Infra-red ray*

Underground tubes. These devices operate on the photo-electric principle in which a current is generated when a light falls onto a photo-electric cell. If the light is interrupted a break occurs in the current and, as in the previous device, the alarm is set off (Figure 17).

When used for alarms the light can be beamed over distances of up to 110 yards (100 metres). It is made invisible (and so not easy to avoid) by passing it through infra-red filters so that it cannot be seen even at night. Obviously the devices themselves should be well concealed from inquisitive potential intruders. If rays are properly installed they form an invisible barrier which is particularly useful along the length of a corridor or across a number of doorways or windows. When used in this way, the infra-red ray forms an effective and reasonably priced detector of considerable re-liability – once fitted and working it seldom gives trouble.

Vibration Detectors. An intruder is almost bound to cause vibration in the structure of a house or flat by breaking a window, forcing a door or climb-ing through a hole in the roof. Devices for detecting this vibration usually rely upon the shaking of a pair of balls or a metal cylinder balanced on contacts carrying the current (Figure 18). When the structure is quite still

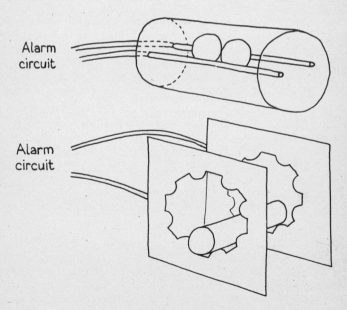

Figure 18. *Types of vibration detector*

the balls (which are usually gold-plated to make a good contact) carry the current from one contact to the other. However, if the place is shaken by the application of a glass cutter on a window or a jemmy levering a door, the balls are shaken off their rails, so breaking the current and starting the alarm sequence.

In order to ensure that these devices only operate when the structure is attacked – and not when there are accidental knocks against the building, including those from rain, hail and other environmental factors – an additional piece of equipment called an 'analyser' should always be used with vibration detectors. The analyser takes the information from a number of detectors and allows the alarm to be operated only when it is satisfied that the vibration has been caused by what it, electronically, recognizes as an intruder.

Movement Detectors. A number of devices can be used to detect the movement of an intruder once he has got into a room. The three most often used operate on one or more of the following principles:

a. Microwave;
b. Ultrasonic;
c. Passive infra-red.

The microwave unit emits a very high frequency radio signal beamed in a fan shape into the room. It receives back the reflected signal and compares it with what was sent out. Anyone moving in the room at a reasonable pace will cause a disturbance of the returned signal which will then trigger the alarm system (Figure 19a). But it should be noted that microwave signals can to some extent penetrate windows, thin walls and doors, so unless these devices are properly sited they may well pick up legitimate movements taking place outside the space they are supposed to be guarding. They do, however, cover good-sized areas and are reliable in operation.

The ultrasonic device also sends out a signal and receives a reflected one back which it compares for any disturbance (Figure 19b). The signal, however, is a very high pitched sound which most people are unable to hear. It is similar to the sound made by special dog whistles, and it is caused by a crystal device called a transducer. The ultrasonic energy is carried on the air and hard surfaces will bounce it back well, while soft furnishings, deep pile carpets and heavy curtains will tend to absorb it and reduce the coverage of the detector. But the most important aspect to remember is that any major movement of air in the room, such as from central heating being suddenly switched on hard near the device, or a draught, may be 'seen' by an ultrasonic device and could cause it to start the alarm.

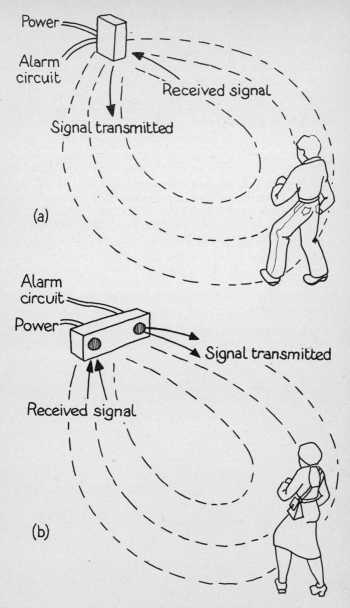

Power

Alarm
circuit

Received signal

Signal transmitted

(a)

Alarm
circuit

Power

Signal transmitted

Received signal

(b)

Figure 19. (*a*) *Microwave detector* (*b*) *Ultrasonic detector*

A report in the Evening Standard read:

A burglar was neatly copped in London the other night. He had broken into the social club to get money from a one-armed bandit in the only infallible way – by forcing open the back of the machine with a jemmy. With the jackpot heavy in his pocket he opened the door to creep away from the premises – and found the police waiting for him outside. The man did not know that the club room was covered by an invisible 'web' of ultrasonic sound – a noise so high pitched that it was inaudible to human ears. This instrument transmits a cone of ultrasonic sound designed to 'recognize' its surroundings and notice any change in the pattern. As soon as the burglar moved, the invisible web was disturbed and the alarm transmitted.

This report describes the principles in good simple terms. The device is a good movement detector when properly used, but the chances of false alarms from air movements or even a telephone in the room should be appreciated before you have it installed. Its area of cover will generally be smaller than that of the microwave device, but it should be slightly less expensive.

The third of these movement detectors, the passive infra-red device, has a very sensitive heat detector at its centre, which detects the heat output, in the infra-red range, from the room and its contents. This sensor sees the infra-red radiations from the walls, furniture, ceiling and floor in the form of a 'picture'. Should an intruder move in the space being guarded, the heat pattern caused by his body coming in front of the original picture will cause the unit to start off the alarm (Figure 20).

The unit is known as passive because it only receives a signal – it does not transmit radio energy like the microwave device, nor any ultrasonic sound which has to come back and be compared. It can cover an area of up to about 33 feet (10 metres) square, which again must not have any rapidly changing heat sources in it – such as a central heating unit close to the device, or the sun or even possibly car headlights shining directly on it. Subject to these considerations, this is a sound and effective device for general use in the detection of the movement of an intruder, costing slightly less than the other two, but considered not of quite such high security.

Which Detector? Only the principal well-proven detectors have been mentioned here. Apart from these there is a wide and bewildering variety available, each one claiming to be the ultimate solution. The one thing you can be certain of is that no single detector is the perfect solution to all problems – whatever the salesman may say. In general it is advisable to stay with devices which are well known and tried, but even here there is a large choice. Which should you use, and where? The usual answer is a variety of devices used in the circumstances which best suit them to do their job

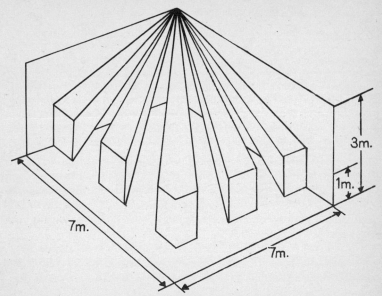

As a person moves from band to band, his motion is sensed as a change in heat in the area.

Figure 20. *Passive infra-red movement detectors: space coverage pattern*

effectively. A professional alarm surveyor will give you a specification setting out his solution, but your knowledge of how you live in your home, as well as your understanding of what each device does, should help you to reach a sensible decision.

As a general guide, magnetic contacts should be used widely – they are cheap and easy to install as well as being thoroughly reliable – but you will have to close all the doors whenever you set the alarm on. Closed circuit wiring is most likely to be appropriate laced around a box covering the safe, or inside the special fur cupboard you may decide on. Pressure pads are a good idea used under carpets near windows which may be used for entry, or even on small landings going upstairs – both places where furniture is not likely to be left inadvertently.

Vibration devices are valuable when used on windows or doors which are likely to be attacked. It is possible to have a complete system of these on the skin of the building which can be left on guard at all times, even when you are using the house – as long as they are switched off to open windows or the back door. Infra-red rays are a good solution to the detection of an intruder likely to move along or across a corridor, and can also cover a row of windows in a long room. In these circumstances they would probably be used in pairs to give height to the invisible barrier.

The movement detectors have applications in rooms containing a reasonable level of valuables. The passive infra-red device would be most suitable for general use, but either ultrasonic or microwave detectors would be more appropriate for a place where very valuable articles were kept. Of course, even when motion detectors were in use, the doors of rooms would have magnetic contacts and perhaps some of the other devices would also be used.

Controls

It is essential that the controls of an alarm system should react only to those messages from the detectors which indicate a real intruder. Consequently, the control itself must be well understood by the users of it. All too often people accidentally trigger their own alarms: at present more than ninety per cent of alarm calls are false and the police quite understandably get tired of responding to them.

The functions of the controls are to:

a. Monitor the system at all times to detect any tampering;
b. Provide power for the whole alarm;
c. Test the system, to ensure that all the detectors are closed and the circuits are clear (i.e. the closed circuit is complete);
d. Switch on the system, to make it live;
e. Allow the operator to leave the premises without setting off the alarm;
f. Trigger the signalling system should an intruder operate the detectors;
g. Allow the operator to return and enter the premises without causing an alarm to go off;
h. Turn the alarm off.

As already said, the circuit needs to be protected from cutting, breaking or tampering, and this should apply at all times in case the system gets interfered with and is then ineffective when called upon.

The power supply – usually of 12 volts – is generally drawn from the mains and transformed to the right voltage with a device like the trickle

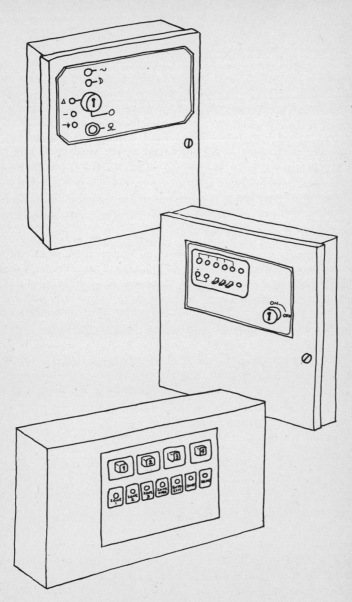

Figure 21. *Examples of controls*

charger for a car battery. This then comes through a rechargeable battery
– for preference – in such a way that should the mains power be cut the
battery will keep the system operating for at least nine hours. If a rechargeable battery is not used, there must be a standby battery of some
kind to which the system will switch automatically and which will give
enough power for the same period of operation. Altogether, the power
supply is the life-blood of the system and should be of the best quality to
ensure that the various parts work smoothly and well.

The process of testing the system will vary with different designs, but in
the simplest there will be a position for the setting switch marked 'Test'.
The setting switch will generally be operated with a key, which should of
course never be left in position in the switch. When the setting switch is
turned to 'Test' there will be indications as to whether or not the system is
clear and ready to be put on. If all doors are shut, furniture off the pressure
pads, nothing in front of the rays and absolute stillness in the rooms containing motion detectors, then the system should indicate an all clear either
by a green light or the lack of a red one or even by a buzzer stopping –
depending on the design. In a large house, the system may be divided into
a number of different circuits, perhaps allocated to different floors, and
each of these circuits will have its own indicator for the Test so that you
can tell where there is something amiss if you do not get a clear showing.
Obviously you must investigate and clear the place where there is a problem
(this may even mean checking all the doors, windows, pads and so on).
This Test position also allows you to try out various parts of the system to
satisfy yourself that they really *do* work: for instance, you can close everything up leaving someone in the room where the pressure pads are and call
out to them to walk on the pads. If the device has worked, the Test light
or indicator should operate. This procedure can be applied to all the detectors on the system – each of the magnetic contacts on doors or windows
as well as any movement detectors there may be. However, you don't need
to try out breaking the wiring!

When the Test has shown all clear, switch the system to ON and take out
the key, keeping it with you. You should then leave your house by the
normal way, called the 'exit route', and there should be some indication,
like a buzzing near the front door, to show that the system is ON. As you
go out of the front door and lock it the buzzing should stop, which tells
you that the whole alarm system is fully set up and ready to identify intruders.

If the alarm operates while you are out, you, or a keyholder you have
nominated (see p. 65), should be called at once. A policeman should
accompany you to the controls to see which part of the system set off the

alarm. Write this down before switching off the alarm, because it's often difficult to remember later. The police should check where the intruder has tried to get in, investigate for fingerprints etc., and make sure you are all-right. Try to get home quickly, as the police may not wait around for you.

Normally, one hopes, the alarm does not go off and you return to your house and open the front door. At once the buzzing sound should start and this reminds you that the alarm is ON. You take out your keys for the system, go to the controls and switch OFF. The buzzer is timed to go on for a limited period, after which the alarm will go off. This is so that if you were forced to open up your house under threats, you could take rather longer than usual fumbling with the keys and so allow the alarm to operate (but it would take a cool nerve!).

Personal Attack Buttons

Another device the controls should have is a connection for personal attack buttons (Figure 22). These are switches which can be used to make the alarm go off at any time – whether it is switched on or not. They should be sited near the front door, in case someone tries to force an entry when you

Figure 22. *Personal attack buttons*

go to answer it; in the main bedroom, in case you hear an intruder in the middle of the night; or at any other point around the house or in the garage where you might suddenly need to call for help. These switches are very simple. They have a mechanical latch to hold them in when they have been pressed and are usually supplied with a simple plastic key, with which to release them after use. Don't leave the key in the personal attack button all the time, otherwise an intruder could switch off the alarm at once. It should also be obvious that these buttons should be mounted well out of reach of children who are likely to press as they ask 'What is *this* for?'

Setting all this out at length should help you to understand the design of your alarm controls and so give you confidence in using them. Above all, make sure that you get clear written instructions on how to use your system, and if there is any aspect you don't understand get the installer to come back and explain it.

Signalling

You will remember that Juno's geese made such a commotion that they managed to rouse the Roman soldiers. An alarm system must achieve the same rousing effect on the police, whose task it is to maintain law and order, as well as the apprehension of intruders on your property. There are two general categories of signalling:

    a. Local warning;
    b. Distance call.

The method used will depend on costs, what is at risk in the house, the area in which the house is situated and even the policy of the local Chief Constable to intruder alarms. But first let us consider what we are talking about.

Local warning. Apart from telephoning the police, the obvious reaction to the discovery of a burglar in your house or flat is to shout as loudly as possible out of the window for help. Such cries are often effective in bringing someone to your aid – as long as you live within earshot (about 55 yards/50 metres) of other people and, of course, they are willing to help. An alarm system can work on the same principle by making a noise with its bell, klaxon, siren or warbler outside the house where it is installed, to such effect that neighbours will call the police to investigate. At the same time another bell or noise-maker should be operating in the house to unnerve the intruder. He will often react by trying to cut off the wiring to the bell outside the house. This should, in fact, cause the bell to operate under its own power as bells usually have a rechargeable battery in their housing for this

Figure 23. *Local bell with flashing light*

very purpose. They are called self-actuating bells, because they are designed to work on their own if they are cut off from the rest of the alarm system.

Another aspect of these local bells is that they should be installed with a 'cut-out' mechanism which will stop them ringing after about twenty minutes. This is so that they do not infringe the law by polluting the area with noise (for which the owner could be prosecuted). If, however, the bell housing also has a flashing light (Figure 23), this can be kept going to indicate that the alarm signal is still operating. The flashing light is also useful to police, who may see the light more quickly than they can hear from which particular house the alarm is sounding.

Distance Call. By using telephone lines a call for help can be sent over any distance, and in a few cases direct to the police. Such methods of signalling use the following:

    a. Automatic '999' machine, through the Post Office emergency service;
    b. Automatic digital machine through to a security company's control station or operations room;
    c. Direct line to the police or the security company's central station or operations room.

The first of these consists of an automatic message-sending machine – usually a tape transmitter – which, when the alarm is triggered by the controls, dials '999' and passes a message such as: 'Police, police, police' and 'This is an X Alarm, suspected intruders entering premises at 123 Quiet Way, Haddit.' When the telephone exchange hears the request for 'police' they put the call through to the police operations room, who in turn take the message and pass instructions to the patrol cars nearest the place in question to investigate the report.

This system achieves a quick and effective response as long as it works properly. Its disadvantage is that if the line used for the alarm is a normal one for the house, the thief could engage the number first from a call box and so prevent the machine from getting through to the exchange. A separate alarm number should therefore be used, which should be specified to the Post Office as for 'outward calls only'. The line should, if possible, be buried or hidden, to prevent the intending burglar cutting it.

An automatic digital machine, which can dial any number it is programmed for, can be used to pass a coded message to a security company. They in turn call the police to the home and, probably, send their own alarm engineer to help if need be. Such an arrangement is particularly useful if the security company have also been entrusted with your keys and so can let the police into the house if you are away. However, as with the automatic '999' machine, there is always the danger of having the line cut or engaged.

The best solution is to have a direct line which is a Post Office 'private wire' from one place to another. With this system the line can be constantly checked and, if cut, will be treated like an alarm by the operations room. However, a private line costs a great deal in rental charges to the Post Office. This may not matter if the contents of the house are very valuable, or if the central station is not more than a couple of miles away. Major companies have overcome this problem to some extent by setting up their own private network of Post Office lines on which they can put many hundreds of alarm signals. This is an effective compromise although the costs need to be studied carefully.

All three parts of the alarm system, the detectors, controls and signalling, must always work properly whenever they are required. It is no good having very sophisticated detector devices connected to poor controls, which are too much trouble to operate and so get left switched off. Equally useless is an excellent system, which only has local warning bells of which no one in the neighbourhood will take any notice.

The Response

When it comes to the Response, we naturally look to the police for help, so it's important that they should be in possession of all the information they need! For a start they need to know that you have had an alarm system installed, so send a note to your local police station telling them you have had an alarm fitted by Company X (or even that you have put it in yourself). The local station will then send you a card to fill in giving them details of your address and type of alarm system and asking you for the names, addresses and telephone numbers of your 'keyholders'. This is very important information and you must get it right and keep it up to date.

When the police respond to an alarm call they can only enter your house if there is a visible sign of entry having been made, i.e. a window broken in or a door forced. Failing such a sign, the police can only check the outside and then wait for you or someone you nominate to arrive with the key and let them in. And if you take too long getting there the police will not wait indefinitely because they are likely to have more important tasks to perform. So when the police are called to answer an alarm, the procedure is to send the patrol car nearest to the house to investigate and at the same time inform the local police station to pass a message to the keyholder to get to the house. In the local station they look at your card and telephone the first keyholder on the list to tell them what has happened. If the keyholder is not in, they will phone the next, and so on. In all, there will be up to four attempts to get someone to the house, but if no one is available the alarm call cannot be properly investigated and the alarm itself will remain ringing – at least in the house. So make sure that you ask close relatives or friends to act as keyholders and, above all, tell them how to get in or out of the house, switch off the alarm and switch it on again.

It is possible to get security companies to act as keyholders for you. They make a contract with you for the service and charge for it, and they also charge for each time they are called out when the alarm goes off. But this does ensure that both the police and a keyholder respond to the alarm when it calls for assistance.

Maintenance

In order to ensure that your alarm system is effective at all times you should not only constantly check it yourself but also have it properly and regularly serviced. The alarm is checked every time you switch the controls to 'Test' and occasionally you should take the trouble to try out the detectors in the way described in the section on Controls above. Apart this checking, the system should be regularly maintained. This will normally be done by the alarm company who installed the system and should be carried out at least twice a year. This maintenance usually includes checking and adjusting each part of the system, including all the detectors, the power supply and batteries and the signalling. Again there is a charge for this – probably in the form of a maintenance contract or, if the system is rented, a rental maintenance contract.

The alarm industry has been one of the most rapidly growing ones over the last decade. As a result a large number of people offer their services as

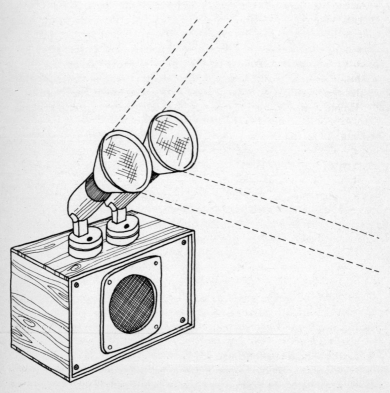

Figure 24. *A free-standing alarm*

installers of alarms who may have little knowledge of the business and who may even be unreliable. The security industry tries to maintain standards through its trade association, but can only do so for its members. As a general rule, therefore, it is wise to deal only with companies who belong to the British Security Industry Association or who are approved by their inspecting organization, the National Supervisory Council for Intruder Alarms. Of course, if you are satisfied with a small local company and have confidence in the staff you will probably get the work done at a more reasonable price, but do be very careful about employing 'cowboys'.

One of the many new developments in the alarm field is the use of radio. This can be applied by giving each detector a tiny radio transmitter and battery with which it communicates to the receiver at the control unit – so doing away with the need for wiring all over the house. While this is an attractive idea, it is not very good security. All the batteries have to be charged at regular intervals or the devices will stop working. At the same time such a system does not 'fail safe' – when something goes wrong it does not sound an alarm as a secure system should. Furthermore, the radio net is subject to outside interference, which is likely to cause false alarms; and finally, Post Office regulations for the use of radio transmitters on this scale would have to be cleared. Such systems have been popular in the United States for many years, but are less likely to gain acceptance here.

A number of free-standing alarms are marketed from time to time. These usually consist of a compact unit containing a detector, usually an ultrasonic type, a mains connection transformer and a standby battery, a switch and timer for setting and finally a local signalling device, like a 'shrieker' or electronic sounder. Again, this equipment is attractive because there is no need to run cabling all over the house, but though such a system is certainly better than no alarm at all, from the proper security aspect it is of little value – even if a floodlight is attached (Figure 24).

Check List

1. Why do you feel you need an alarm system?
2. Would you/do you use the system regularly? If not, why not?
3. Do you know what your insurance requirements are in relation to your alarm?
4. Have you had any false alarms?
5. How do you propose to prevent there being any in the future?
6. Have you told the police you have an alarm and has the Crime Prevention Officer looked at it?

7. Do the listed keyholders still have keys and are they all still willing and able to help?
8. Is your alarm more than ten years old? If so, have the alarm company recommended renewing it?
9. Have you had the alarm modified whenever you had a major change or alteration carried out on your house/flat?
10. Would you recommend your alarm system to close friends?

Chapter 5
Personal Protection

5. Personal Protection

The Risks

As with other security problems, the first consideration in personal protection is to recognize the risks a person is exposed to. These may range from being the victim of a pickpocket, mugger or rapist to intimidation, kidnap or even assassination. Clearly a head of state of a major country faces a risk of assassination at any time and so will have bodyguards or agents to protect him. Some millionaires who are in genuine fear for their lives go further and travel in armour-protected cars, wear bullet-proof vests and disguise themselves as far as possible. Such measures, however, besides being very expensive and difficult to live with, are generally appropriate for very high-risk individuals only.

Once the risks have been recognized, steps should be taken to avoid or at least minimize them. The head of state and certain other personalities cannot avoid the risk of assassination because of the nature of their jobs and so have to be provided with extraordinary security protection. At the other extreme young girls who run away to London and explore the 'seamier' parts of it voluntarily expose themselves to all sorts of dangers. Neither the police nor their parents can protect them in those circumstances and they are unlikely to know how to begin to protect themselves. The following is from a recent report in the *Daily Telegraph*:

> Girls who 'play with fire' by striking up casual acquaintances at late-night discos can only bring themselves trouble, said Mr Alex Rennie, Chief Constable of West Mercia, launching a crime prevention week yesterday. 'They get into conversation too readily with men, casually at discos or on their way home late at night, and then find the situation too hot to handle', he said. 'They don't realize the dangers. Despite the so-called sex equality act they must learn that they cannot switch off as they wish. My message to them is to avoid situations where they are likely to encourage attacks for sexual gratification.'

Your Attitude

Your attitude to protection is of prime importance. When you have considered the risks you are likely to run and how to avoid as many of them as possible you should go on to consider how you can deal positively with the remainder. This doesn't mean seeing villains behind every lamp post or screaming for help at every unidentified noise in the house. A knowledge of the problems and what can be done about them should in fact give you the confidence to live your life fully, without fear and without foolhardiness.

A girl who has learnt karate will have the technique to physically defend herself if necessary, but above all she will have learned the self-discipline to calm herself and think clearly about how she is going to deal with a threatening situation. While not many people will be prepared to study the 'martial arts' or self-defence, everyone should understand the importance of achieving a calm and determined state of mind in the face of a potential attack.

In Paul Scott's novel *The Jewel in the Crown* – part of *The Raj Quartet* (Morrow, 1978) – he recounts the story (based on a true case) of a schoolteacher who was to remember the occasion for which she received a presentation for her courage:

> All she had done was to stand on the threshold of the schoolhouse, into which she had already herded the children, and deny entry – in fluent Urdu, using expressions she could hardly have repeated to her superiors – to a detachment of half-hearted rioters. At least, she assumed they were half-hearted, although later, only an hour later, they or more determined colleagues, sacked and burned the Catholic mission house down the road . . .

The perverseness of attitude which, in spite of being outnumbered, outarmed or whatever, just does not see why you should be bullied, pushed around or attacked is a great defence against aggression. It may not be successful in itself, but if there is no escaping the danger, it will be enormously helpful in the next stage, which is that you fight if you absolutely have to. Methods of self-defence are described on p. 76ff., but it is worth stressing here that you should be prepared to really hurt your attacker as he comes at you. The slap to the face or the flailing arms are worse than useless, for they will tend only to excite the bully and give him a sense of power. If you are under attack and cannot escape, then commit yourself to damaging the aggressor so badly that he will have to let you go – no more and no less.

So the attitude you need to develop – and like all attitude-changes it does not come at once, but gets built up gradually – is made up of the following:

a. Awareness of your surroundings, so that you can recognize the possibility of real danger before it is upon you;

b. The confidence in yourself to run away rather than the need to show how brave you are;

c. If there really is no escape, then the calming determination that you will not be bullied or attacked;

d. Finally, should you be attacked, the commitment to plan and carry out wholeheartedly the self-defence action which will so hurt the aggressor that you can escape.

Petty Theft

Although there are some really expert pickpockets ('dips') and bag-snatchers, and even underworld schools (as in *Oliver Twist*) where the skills are taught, the great majority of these crimes are committed by opportunists or casual thieves. Millions of pounds a year are stolen in this way and very little of it is recovered by the owners. The classic examples of victims are men who carry their wallets in the back hip-pocket of their trousers and women with open handbags – particularly in crowded conditions, such as tube trains (Figure 25). Not all thieves are men: there are many female pickpockets, especially in markets and on public transport; some are convicted of violent robbery – not only against other women.

Without getting anxious about it, just think constructively how to pre-

Never leave your handbag open.
A 'dip' could get at the contents
without you feeling a thing.

Thousands of wallets
are lost every year by men
who carry them like this.

Figure 25. *Good targets for pickpockets*

vent these items from being stolen. In a crowded train keep an arm across your chest when the wallet is in your inside breast pocket, particularly just as you arrive at a station (that is the time the thief is most likely to snatch and escape on to the platform). In the case of a handbag, hold it close to you, as well as putting your arm through its handle if it has one and, again, be particularly on guard in crowded places. In certain cities, such as Rome, a woman does better not to carry a bag at all when she is in the street, while in New York there has been an epidemic of tearing gold chains from girls' necks, whatever the injury caused in the process. Remember always that the thief has no compunction in reacting violently and has no consideration or compassion for you.

If you have to carry a lot of cash around, such as when on holiday, a

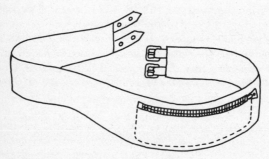

Figure 26. *Money Belt*

sensible precaution is to wear an old-fashioned money belt (Figure 26). Ideally the belt should be fixed around the waist under your clothes. By keeping a smaller quantity of money in your purse or wallet, you should only need to get at your money belt once or twice a day. The amount at risk is thus kept to the minimum and the main part of your resources are well hidden and secured.

The wearing of expensive jewellery in public places offers the casual thief, and sometimes the professional, a challenge which he can seldom resist. If you must wear expensive rings, at least twist them so that the jewels are towards your palms until you arrive at where they need to be seen. Diamond tie-pins and brooches should also be kept covered with a scarf or coat until the time when they really need to be shown off.

While jewellery is an obvious target, the implications of losing a wallet, notecase or handbag can be even more serious. Many lessons can be drawn from the case of a middle-aged woman who lost her bag while shopping in a famous London store. She went to the cloakroom of the store and put her bag on the floor for a moment while she adjusted her clothing; as she bent to pick up the bag she found it had gone – snatched. She rushed out of the cloakroom but could see no one whom she could reasonably accuse, so she went to the security office and reported her loss there. The police investigated without success and she was eventually helped to her home and let into her house by her son as she no longer had the keys. Apart from the money she had lost, the lack of credit cards, diary, address book and favourite make-up all caused her considerable distress. About three days later she had a telephone call which delighted her: 'This is the store's security office. We've found your handbag hidden in a cupboard near the stairways. The money's gone but all the rest seems all right. When would you like to collect it?' She said she would come at once. It took her half an hour to get to the store and the security office denied all knowledge of finding her bag or of telephoning her. With this disappointment, her journey home was miserable but when she went in through the front door she thought the world had gone mad – the whole place had been ransacked and her most valuable pieces of furniture had been removed! Obviously, the handbag thieves had set up the operation, knew exactly how long they had to do their work, and as she went down the street, drove a van to her front door and did their worst.

There are an appalling number of similar stories. Their moral is to be particularly on guard if you are unfortunate enough to have your handbag or wallet stolen. Keep a note at home of the number of your credit cards (and cheque card) and the telephone numbers you should call if they get lost.

Assault, Robbery and Rape

In discussing these crimes we move on into an area which makes 'ordinary' thieving seem almost pleasant by comparison. It is important to emphasize again that the development of an awareness of danger is the most valuable asset. Next, always remember that it is far better to run away to safety than prove how brave you are. In wartime it used to be said that there were plenty of old or bold pilots, but not both. This may appear ungallant, but it was a fact that the foolhardy type of boldness was a danger to all concerned. If you have qualms about going along a particular street late at night then do not go along it alone. Call a friend or go another way. If you see a gang of youths coming towards you on the pavement, it is not worth demonstrating to them that you have as much right to be walking there as they have – cross to the other side of the road and carry on, unimpressed by their childish need to express aggression. If you have reason to believe you are being followed make your way to the nearest house where there is a sign of life, explain your predicament and ask if you can wait there awhile. The variations on the theme are endless, but the essential to remember is to avoid the danger you have sensed rather than face it unnecessarily.

Assaults, robberies with violence and rape are real threats to most people at some stage of their lives. Many cases are unpremeditated: the burglar who is caught in the act is likely to react violently through fear; and if his discoverer is a girl, she will be at considerable risk unless she is very cool and knows what she is doing. The youths who decide to mug the next passer-by may well be showing off to each other or to their girlfriends. On the other hand, the man who knocks a schoolteacher off her bicycle on the lonely lane she always rides along after her late class has built strange fantasies for himself and the teacher, which he is determined to put into practice.

In each the potential victim has a few moments in which to take control of the situation – or lose it. As said earlier, to take control requires calm confidence and the perverse determination not to be 'bullied'. In most cases this is possible provided you take time to think clearly and know that you can and will win through to safety. The ability to think comes largely from disciplining yourself to breathe deeply and steadily. Most people's reaction to being afraid is to hold their breath, so preventing the flow of oxygen, carried in the blood, from getting to the brain and also to body muscles. The result can be a form of mental and physical paralysis. By deliberately breathing in through the nose and out through the mouth you should be able to collect your thoughts and take control. Remember that your attackers will probably also be tense at that moment and holding their breath!

The knowledge that, in the ultimate situation, you will win through to safety will come from your ability to defend yourself. Unfortunately the art of self-defence is far too seldom taught in our society. In all animal species except modern man, the young learn self-defence and survival as part of their play. They learn to know their natural weapons like claws and teeth, speed and weight, as well as how to avoid predators. If you have learned self-defence you will have the confidence to know that you really can win through to safety. As a result, you will be able to handle the situation calmly and perhaps talk yourself out of trouble.

Self-Defence

In a proposed assault or rape the attacker is driven by strong emotions which are not easy to combat. Above all, no ideas of what is fair or foul will enter the situation – and his victim should have no compunction in hurting him sufficiently to be able to escape.

The weapons everyone has available are the hard parts of the limbs and body; striking with them will not hurt you. They are:

- Head – to butt with;
- Teeth – to bite with;
- Edges of palms of hands – which are far stronger than bare fists;
- Pointed fingers or thumbs – to stab with;
- Elbows – to strike backwards or to the side;
- Knees – to strike upwards;
- Heels – to strike downwards or backwards.

Then consider the 'target' areas where the attacker will be most sensitive to each application:

- Eyes – stab;
- Nose – strike or stab up and twist or bite;
- Mouth – strike;
- Below the ears – strike;
- Throat – strike;
- Inside of collarbone – stab;
- Solar plexus – strike;
- Elbow – strike;
- Genitals – strike, twist, squeeze;
- Knees – strike below;
- Inside leg – pinch hard;
- Instep – strike (stamp).

These are illustrated in terms of a woman defending herself against a male attacker in Figure 27. The 'weapons' used are the same whatever your sex, but the target areas will vary a bit. A woman's genital area is not as sensitive as that of a man, but the breasts and lower abdomen are additional target areas.

As these lists demonstrate, there is plenty of scope for determined defenders to render a good account of themselves. Real confidence in self-defence comes from study and practice over many months, which is best carried out in a class under expert tuition. But a basic knowledge of how to use the 'weapons' could be invaluable. Trying to remember various stances and positions you may have read about will be of little help in an emergency. The essential is to react instinctively, at the right time, with the most effective combination of 'weapons' and target.

In addition, remember that noise can be unnerving to an intruder or

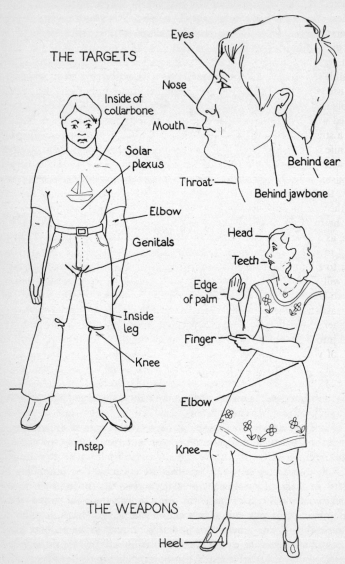

THE TARGETS

Eyes

Nose

Inside of collarbone

Mouth

Solar plexus

Behind ear

Elbow

Throat

Behind jawbone

Genitals

Head

Teeth

Edge of palm

Inside leg

Finger

Knee

Elbow

Instep

Knee

THE WEAPONS

Heel

Figure 27. *A woman defending herself against a male attacker*

attacker. At the same time as you use any of the 'weapons', let out the loudest cry or roar you can manage. This will not only surprise and, maybe, unnerve your attacker, but also give you additional strength and confidence you did not know you had.

In general don't try to deal with an attacker at a distance – this is only possible if you have a strong chain, with a bunch of keys on it, which you can use as a mace. Let the attacker begin the proceedings while you breathe deeply and plan how you will deal with him. For example, if the attacker is armed with a pistol or a knife or even a broken bottle you are unlikely to win a straight fight – so work out what you will do when he puts the pistol or knife to one side. Until that point, comply with what he tells you to do, but without making it any easier for him than you have to. When he puts the pistol in his pocket or the knife on one side in order to take what he is after, that is the moment to let him come close and strike him. In this case jab the middle fingers of your hands hard and straight into his eyes – so that he can't see to shoot you – and then use your knee to strike him as hard as you can in the genitals – so that he can't follow you. Then get away to safety as quickly as possible and whatever you do, do NOT look back to admire your workmanship. You have either done the job properly and will not be worried further or you were half-hearted in what you did and so almost deserve the awful consequences (and they really will be very unpleasant, so there are absolutely no half measures in this business).

Other methods of striking an attacker from the front are to butt your head into his face, making sure you break his nose; hit upwards with the edge of your palm at his throat or nose; hit hard with your knee into his solar plexus; kick with your heel at his knee, when his leg is straight, or down on the instep of his foot – with all your weight and strength. But always remember that you are making sure that you can get away to safety, not trying to inflict revenge.

The girl who discovers a burglar in her flat may be in her nightdress or even in bed when he comes into the room. Unless she is successful at talking him out of the flat, there is a strong possibility that he will try to rape her, threatening her with whatever he is carrying to intimidate her further. In these circumstances the procedure is far harder to remember and even more difficult to carry out. But she has somehow got to remain calm, breathing deeply, and plan how and when to deal with the man. He will undoubtedly throw her down so that she cannot strike with her knees; but he will put down the club or knife he was threatening her with while he opens or removes his trousers. When he gets on top of her his attention will be diverted to his genitals, so this is the moment to strike with all her strength at his eyes or nose. She can put her hands to the sides of his head

– as if the act was lovemaking – and then jab her thumbs into his eyes. Alternatively, she can put her hands behind his head and bring it forward as she violently butts his nose with her forehead. If her hands are pinned down she will have to wait for the right moment to butt his face. Whichever course she adopts, she should let out a loud shriek and roll free. She should then strike quickly and decisively once more, probably with her knee or the edge of her palm, or stamp her heel very hard into his genitals or his face. She should then get out of the flat and into a neighbour's as quickly as possible.

Of course, every case of attempted rape is different, but women can very often defend themselves successfully if they have the necessary knowledge and determination.

The schoolteacher who is knocked off her bicycle is probably in great danger of being murdered, though rape may be an 'incidental'. If talking to her attacker proved inadequate, she would have to use all available 'weapons' quickly. If her attacker approached from the side, she should swing her elbow horizontally into his solar plexus or up at his throat; if she could swing round sufficiently, she might be able to drive her far knee into his genitals. If she has been knocked to the ground, she should wait for the assailant to get close, and then butt him in the face with her head, jab his eyes with her fingers or thumbs, or strike him in the genitals with her heel or knee. In either case, she would require a combination of two of these strikes to incapacitate him enough to make her escape.

There is no way in which one can satisfactorily teach self-defence from a book, but it is important to appreciate that there is usually no inevitability about being a victim. If you cannot or will not go to classes to learn how to defend yourself, then at least do the following:

a. Keep fit – whatever your age: take exercise and eat and drink in moderation;
b. Recognize your 'weapons' and try them out by jabbing your finger or thumb into a pillow and striking with the edge of your palm, your elbow, knee and heel with all your strength at a mattress. Practise too the loudest shriek or cry you can manage – preferably somewhere you won't alarm or disturb anyone else.
c. Study the target areas on people around you and work out how close you would have to be to them to strike hard (obviously, don't practise it, except under expert tuition in a class). Remember that you have to be close to all the targets to be effective.

Additional Weapons. A few generations ago girls were taught that their best weapon of defence was a hat pin. As these were sharp, steel objects at least 6 inches (15 cm) long, they could obviously have been very effective as daggers. Today, however, the carrying of such a pin would probably be against the law. The legal position is that you may not carry an offensive weapon – even only for defensive purposes. This means you may not have on you when you go out in public – without a specific licence – a gun, pistol, long-bladed knife, sword-stick, truncheon, knuckle duster, acid, ammonia or gas sprays, and so on – in fact anything which might be used to attack or threaten another person. There are, however, a number of things carried normally and legitimately which can be of considerable help in an emergency – provided that you have thought about it and practised using them beforehand.

Earlier mention was made of keys on a chain – this can be a very effective weapon if kept close to hand and used with skill. Wielding it like a mace can make a number of aggressors stand back, but if you consider having this in your 'armoury', do practise using it so that you will know what you are doing when you take it out in earnest. A bunch of keys held in the fist can also make a good additional weapon of defence: with the bunch in your palm and the longest (probably the car key) protruding between your fingers, you can stop someone very sharply by jabbing the single key up his nose or at any other part of his face (Figure 28).

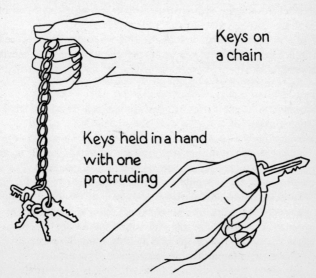

Keys on
a chain

Keys held in a hand
with one
protruding

Figure 28. *Keys as weapons*

Other items, such as pointed scissors, spray cans of hair lacquer or toilet water, or a ballpoint pen may be useful if you can get at them quickly in an emergency. Remember that umbrellas should be jabbed at short range – it's a waste of time beating anyone with them. In all cases these articles should be applied to the target areas described earlier.

'Shriek Alarm' is a proprietary article which is extensively sold, and consists of a very small air hooter operated by a small gas cylinder used to charge certain refillable soda syphons. When the operating button of this device is pressed it will produce an ear-piercing noise for about thirty seconds. This can be helpful in the event of attack or threatened attack, but, once again, must be close to hand. A whistle may be carried on a cord or chain around the neck, but as with other alarms, who is going to hear it and above all will anyone *do* anything about it?

Threats

Some criminals use threats to achieve their goal with the minimum danger and the least effort. There are also a number of unbalanced people who get a form of excitement and fulfilment by threatening others. Treat all of them the same way – as criminals attempting a form of assault. As such, the same rules apply: avoid the danger if you can, have the confidence in yourself to brush it aside, but if it has to be dealt with know how to do so and where you can turn to for help. In nearly every situation the answer is to tell the police, supplying them with as much information as possible. In the case of verbal threats, write down as soon as possible where and at what time the threat was delivered and the exact words used. Don't worry about having to write down language which may revolt or horrify you. Then give this record to the police, together with names and addresses of any witnesses of the event. Written threats can be passed directly to the police – complete with the envelope and as little handling as possible.

The telephone gives a direct form of access into your house for anyone who is prepared to spend the money on a call. This means that a number of threatening and dirty telephone calls are being made regularly. A point to emphasize is that if a subscriber's entry in the directory indicates that she is a woman, she will almost certainly get obscene telephone calls from time to time. The origin of calls can sometimes be traced by the Post Office, but the caller needs to be kept talking while the supervisor at the exchange is alerted on another line, and this is often impossible. The best plan, particularly if you are a woman on your own, is to stick to the following rules:

Telephoned Threat Report

KEEP CALLER TALKING — DO NOT INTERRUPT

ORIGIN OF CALL

Local ☐   Long Distance ☐   Call Box ☐   Internal ☐

If internal call – leave plug in switchboard.

For other calls – employ line seizure equipment (if any) to hold circuit and trace other calls.

Callers identity: Male/Female*   Estimated age group_____

Did caller sound familiar with the aircraft or building by his description of the bomb location? Yes/No*

*Delete as necessary

VOICE			
1. Loud ☐	3. Raspy ☐		
Soft ☐	Pleasant ☐		
2. High Pitched ☐	4. Intoxicated ☐		
Deep ☐	Normal ☐		
Other_____			

ACCENT

Foreign ☐	Race_____
Local ☐	
Not Local ☐	Region_____

SPEECH

Fast ☐	Distinct ☐
Slow ☐	Distorted ☐
Slurred ☐	Stutter ☐
Nasal ☐	Other_____

MANNER			
1. Calm ☐	4. Obscene ☐
Angry ☐	Courteous ☐
2. Coherent ☐	5. Laughing ☐
Incoherent ☐	Serious ☐
3. Emotional ☐	6. Rational ☐
Unemotional ☐	Irrational ☐

COMMAND OF LANGUAGE

Excellent ☐	Fair ☐
Good ☐	Poor ☐
Other_____	

BACKGROUND NOISE

None ☐	Mixed ☐
Loud ☐	Other Voices ☐

Other (aircraft, machines, trains, animals etc.)

ACTION – Immediately after call, notify the following persons in order:

1. Police	Tel No._____	4_____	Tel No._____
2. Security Officer	Tel No._____	5_____	Tel No._____
3_____	Tel No._____	6_____	Tel No._____

Figure 29. *Telephoned Threat Report: Keep a sheet made out like this near the telephone*

a. Don't talk to anyone of whom you are doubtful. Don't give them the audience they want;
b. Hang up at the first obscene word, or if the caller doesn't say anything (for instance, heavy breathing), or doesn't identify himself to your satisfaction;
c. Call the supervisor at the exchange (100) if the calls persist.

Another way to help trace the caller is to find out as much as you can about him and where the call is coming from: note his accent, the words and expressions he uses, his possible age, and listen for any background noises such as traffic, trains, aircraft taking off, people's voices in a pub and so on. Again, write all this down, as well as the exact time of the call, so that the police and Post Office will have something to work with. If you have a tape recorder near by you could also try recording the calls and then tell the caller you have done so. If he believes you, you are unlikely to be troubled by that particular individual again.

The process of tracing the call clearly takes on vital proportions in the case of bomb threats or threats of kidnap or assassination. For while the voice on the telephone mouthing obscenities may seem funny, sad, or just tiresome, when someone says 'we have just picked up your child from school and it will cost you £10,000 to see her again in one piece', the joke is certainly over. So learn to listen 'professionally' to all anonymous calls. You may find it helpful to have a sheet of paper near the telephone made out as shown in Figure 29.

Hostages and Kidnap

In many areas of the world kidnap and hostage-taking have become the regular routine of criminal gangs or terrorists. They have found the kidnapping of their 'targets' comparatively easy and the returns on their efforts most rewarding. Many people think that such crimes happen only in South America, Italy or the USA, but this is just not so. There have been several in the UK in the last few years and the tendency is for the numbers to increase. Hostage-taking and threatening is a very prevalent crime in the USA, but the American police have an enviable record of success in freeing victims, with virtually no loss of life. Success like this persuades the criminal gangs that there may be easier ways of relieving the public of large sums of money. The record in this country has been less consistent and the danger of an increase in these crimes is therefore very real.

Moreover, it is not only the very rich, the outspoken politician, or the well-known personage who become victims. People can be taken hostage simply because they are at a certain place at a certain time – as in the case of Balcombe Street in the late 1970s, when the victims were just sitting in their flat minding their own business. Others even get kidnapped by mistake – in one case the victim's name was the same as a more likely target's and she was never seen again.

The circumstances of a hostage situation are usually so much a matter of chance that it may be difficult to avoid. However, as always, the first thing to do is to collect yourself and think clearly. If you can do this and remain uninfluenced by the general panic of the other people in, say, a bank when it is raided, you may be the one person near the stairs able to escape without being noticed. That first minute is the critical one for the raiders and their victims, and if escape is not possible at the outset it will become increasingly difficult when guarding routines have been properly established.

If there is no escape and you are held as a hostage the dangers you will have to face will be both physical and psychological. The fact that you are in the hands of someone who has the power of life or death over you can have a very traumatic effect. The results vary considerably – from what is known as the Stockholm Syndrome, when certain victims fall in love with and eventually marry their captors, to the euphoric behaviour of the Iranian diplomats when rescued by the SAS in 1980. Avoiding the extreme psychological effects is possible by self-discipline and a logical planning of one's mental activities. Many books have been written on the subject, from Victor Hugo's *Les Misérables* to Sir Geoffrey Jackson's *Surviving the Long Night*, and though they are separated by nearly two hundred years the techniques used by the victims to survive mentally are comparable. The essential is to keep your brain active – working out, planning, calculating and testing so that it does not get subjugated and destroyed by the experience.

At the same time a similar process should be applied to your body. Whatever the circumstances of your captivity, whether bound and gagged or not, you must try to deliberately exercise all the muscles of your body regularly. If you have had any training in Yoga or other techniques of muscle control this will prove invaluable. Again, what is required is the determination not to be physically incapacitated. If you look after both mind and body in this way, you will have gained a degree of control.

Much more positive measures can be taken to avoid being kidnapped. If you feel there is a possibility that you or any member of your family might be subjected to this it is worth taking professional advice from either the police or security consultants. They will give you detailed procedures, which will apply to your particular circumstances. These are almost certain to include the following:

a. Avoid, as far as possible, a regular routine going to and from work;
b. Be aware of any suspicious circumstances which could develop dangerously;
c. Have all the people who work for you security checked;
d. Make sure your wife's and children's activities are known about by someone in the family's confidence;
e. Ensure that members of your family never accept lifts or spontaneously go out with strangers;
f. Have your house or flat checked for its security and ensure that you have a good alarm;
g. Have a sound control of anyone who is allowed to enter your house.

These steps are comparatively easy to incorporate and perfectly valid security measures for most people to take. In particular, be aware of the possibility of danger in certain circumstances.

If the worst occurs, and you or a member of your family is taken, with the usual warning that 'you cause their death if you go to the police – we are watching you' – what should be done? There are obviously no ready solutions to every situation, but generally the rules are as follows:

a. Do whatever you believe is necessary to save the victim's life: this does *not* include paying the money or doing what is demanded at once. You show willing, but keep as much as possible of what they want in your hands to bargain with;
b. You insist that a negotiator be appointed on your side, so that you can get on with finding the money or whatever excuse you can think of. Have your family solicitor (if he has a strong personality) or someone similar take on this role. His function will be to drag out the negotiations until the criminals are found. Because he is not directly emotionally involved he will be a far better negotiator than one of the family;
c. You ensure that the police and perhaps a professional security advisor know of what is happening and help you to solve the problem.

Obviously the situation has to be handled with great skill and courage. But whether you are a bank manager, or have won the football pools you are as likely to be a target as a successful businessman driving around in his Rolls Royce. So be prepared mentally, talk about it with your wife, and establish a simple code word you could use to each other in an emergency: then ask your solicitor or best friend to be prepared to act as negotiator should he ever be required, and look to your own and your family's security arrangements.

Check List

1. Do you think you can recognize a situation which is potentially dangerous for you and are you prepared to avoid it – if necessary to run away?
2. Do you keep yourself fit for your age, with plenty of exercise and with moderate eating and drinking? If not, do you realize what a 'soft' victim you would be?
3. Do you ever find you have been walking around with your bag open or have left your wallet in a jacket hanging on the back of a chair in your office? Do you feel guilty of a security breach and of having offered temptation to others?
4. In a crowd, are you always conscious of the valuables you carry? Do you hold on to them as tightly as possible?
5. If you carry a cheque book, will it be possible for a pickpocket to steal both it and the cheque card at the same time? If so, do you realize how much money they can draw from banks in a matter of hours and do you know whom to notify of the loss?
6. What will you do if you see someone 'dipping' into a woman's handbag in front of you in the train? Do you create a fuss and what *can* you do, or do you pretend you didn't see? Similarly, what is your reaction to seeing a man molesting a girl in the crowd you are in?
7. What will you do if two people corner you in a dark part of the road home and demand your money?
8. What is your reaction to an obscene telephone call? What if it is a threatening one?
9. If you were kidnapped, would anyone in your family know how to help or what to do?
10. Do you feel that the police are there to help you and really will do so if you give them the help they need? Does this apply in all situations – or only the ones in which you feel *you* are at risk?

Chapter 6
Looking After Your Goods and Chattels

6. Looking After Your Goods and Chattels

Surveillance

In St Albans cathedral you can still see where the sacred relics were placed, to be viewed by pilgrims of bygone ages. These relics were on show in special cases in the centre of the viewing chamber where the pilgrims could walk around them. Behind the people, as they gazed in rapt devotion, was a raised gallery, boxed in, with slits cut in the panels through which the monks maintained a watchful eye on the treasures – and on the pilgrims!

This process of looking after what you wish to preserve is common today with guardsmen outside Buckingham Palace, commercial security men at art galleries and even a shepherd watching over his flock. Obviously you cannot stand guard over your possessions in the same way, but you will probably check them from time to time or when some incident attracts your attention and prompts you to take a look.

If you have a garden, however small, you will look at it and walk around it not only to enjoy what is growing there but also to make sure that all is in order – that cows have not broken in and trampled the strawberry bed, that cats have not dug up the newly planted bulbs and, maybe, that human intruders have not been in to get at your garage, tool shed or to test out the back windows. Similarly you will sometimes check the front of your house or flat to see what is happening there, and if someone knocks or rings the front-door bell you will find out who it is by looking out of the front window, through a viewing device or just by opening the front door.

In Georgian times, at the beginning of the last century, when homes in Bath, Edinburgh and London often had their sitting room on the first floor, it was a common practice to have a mirror mounted on the window sill in which anyone at the front door could be seen. Such mirrors can still be found in parts of Edinburgh and even on older flats around the Covent Garden area of London (Figure 30). Although, in the 1800s, one function of the mirrors may have been to check bona fide visitors before the occupant decided to be 'at home', the present application is even more important from the security point of view. It is essential that you somehow check who is at the front door before you open it to them.

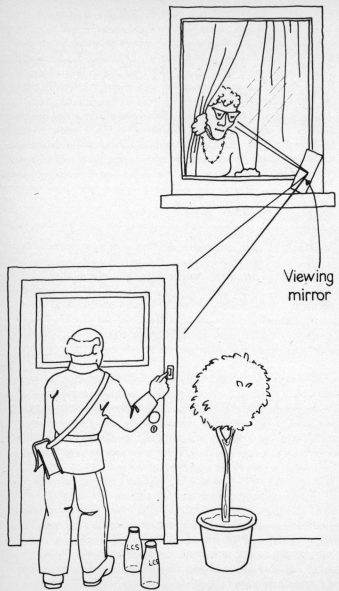

Figure 30. *Surveillance by use of mirrors*

The technique of watching over things in this way is known as surveillance. Clearly, the simplest form of surveillance is to have a small window in the front door, but this can physically weaken the door as well as allowing people to look straight in and inspect the inside of your house. Although the glass can be strengthened with the application of a reflective film of shatterproof material as well as made difficult to see through from outside, it is better security to have a door of good solid construction. With the solid door, the simplest and most economical method of checking the caller is to install a viewing device in the door about 5 feet (1½ metres) from the floor. There are a number of these devices which consist of a metal tube about ⅜ inch (10 mm) in diameter, with a metal cover on the inside and a series of optical convex lenses which should give you a

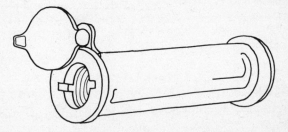

Figure 31. *Door viewer*

wide field of view on the outside (Figure 31). These devices are very easy to install and of great value – as long as you get into the habit of always using them. When there is a ring at the door, open the viewer and see who is there – it really only takes a few seconds – and open the door only if you are satisfied with what you have seen. If not, then call out and ask what the person wants. It is far easier to argue a difficult subject with someone you don't want in your house through a closed door.

Cameras

Closed-circuit television (CCTV) provides an even more sophisticated method of surveillance. With a CCTV system you can check your front door, your garden or any part of the outside of your house, and all that is required is a small TV camera (and they can be very small – comparable with the home-movie cine camera) and a co-axial cable connecting it to your television screen. The co-axial cable is of the same type which is

Figure 32. *T V in sitting room*

connected to the television aerial, so if you give power to the camera and TV set you can have your own CCTV surveillance system. Although the principles are as simple as this, there are other factors to consider: the camera itself needs to be carefully sited, and if it is to be mounted outdoors, it will require a special housing to protect it from the weather. You may have noticed that the cameras which are mounted high up over traffic coming into big cities have their own heated box, on the front of which is a window with a windscreen wiper. They can be operated by remote control to look all around the area and use telescopic lenses to 'zoom in' on a particular object. Such cameras cost thousands of pounds and would only be appropriate for someone who had extensive grounds and employed a number of people to look after them. The advantage of such a system is that one person can operate a number of cameras, some of which may be remotely controlled, to give a far wider area of surveillance than would ever be possible except with an array of employees – and without worrying about the weather.

A CCTV system for supervising the front door can be connected in such a way that when the doorbell is rung your TV set is automatically switched on and the picture of the caller shown (Figure 32). If you are already

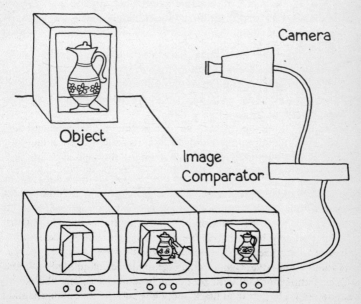

Figure 33. *A CCTV device used as a motion detector*

watching a programme on the TV, this system will show the picture of the caller in the corner of the screen.

A CCTV device can also be used as a motion detector in an alarm system. In this case the camera would be looking at a completely static scene and the picture would be transmitted as an electronic 'package' to a memory device in a comparator. Should something move in the picture, the electronic package will differ from the one already in the memory, so the comparator is alerted and sounds an alarm signal. When you come to investigate, the machine will show you three pictures in turn – first, the original scene, second, what caused the alarm to go off, i.e. the picture with the intruder, and finally, the present situation. The pictures can be shown consecutively on a single screen or simultaneously on three separate ones (Figure 33). Again, such a sophisticated device is appropriate where the item at risk is of considerable value: the advantage of having a record of what caused the incident and, perhaps, an image of the intruder can be of considerable assistance in solving the crime.

A very much more economical method of obtaining a likeness of a suspected wrong-doer is to use photographic cameras, adapted for security purposes. These can use 8 mm, 16 mm or 32 mm film in either colour or black and white, and an 8 mm camera with colour film will cost about a tenth of the amount needed for a CCTV installation with video recorder. Such photographic cameras can be used in one of three ways:

a. Time lapse, where the camera is set to take a frame or picture every so often – for instance, once every half minute. If the camera is used only in daylight hours a roll of film will last a number of days;

b. Continuous running, when the camera will be activated by an emergency and take a whole roll of film;

c. Individual frame operation, when the camera will take a single shot in certain circumstances: for instance, if connected to a contact on a door it could photograph who was coming through each time that door was opened (Figure 34).

This kind of photography can be used to give you an idea of the activity in a certain area, such as your front garden or by the garage door, or perhaps to trap someone you suspect of pilfering from you. The running costs of a photographic installation are not as great as might be expected because you only need to develop those films which cover periods you want to study. The advantage of being able to film in colour is considerable when the identification of a suspect is at issue – and colour film for an 8 mm camera is cheaper than black and white because of the huge market for home movies.

Figure 34. *CCTV device: individual frame operation*

Lighting

In order to see the object you are looking after or at, not only must it be in your field of vision (or that of your surveillance devices) but it must also be adequately illuminated. To peer through a door viewer and see only a shadow in the darkness outside is of little use to you. So make sure there is sufficient light outside your front door for you to recognize a caller and if necessary install a light you can switch on from inside. A light which comes on when the front-door bell is operated may seem a good idea, but it wastes power during daylight and can be a temptation to small boys wanting to 'try out' the system.

There is of course a similar need for lighting when CCTV is used. When there is lighting in the area, such as a street lamp, then a light directly associated with the CCTV camera is probably the most satisfactory arrangement. As such, the light can be automatically adjusted to give a varying amount of illumination according to the lighting required by the camera.

Apart from illuminating a caller, lights used outside the house can act as a very real deterrent to prospective intruders by making it difficult for them to approach the house undetected. In some cases floodlights are left on all night, but they can also be automatically switched on when the house alarm goes off or manually switched on and off as you require them. Apart from their security function, such lights can provide attractive illumination for your garden or backyard when you have parties.

The layout of every house or flat will of course be different, but you should aim at a combination of lighting which will illuminate a caller to the

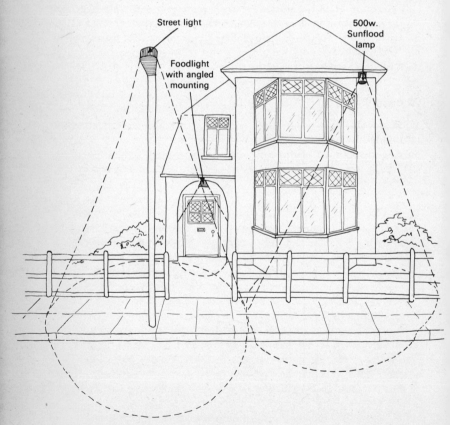

Figure 35. *Lighting the outside of your house*

front door and which will give good cover of the back of the house and garden. For the front door, a spotlight mounted above the door bell, about 10 feet (3 metres) from the ground, would give good illumination of anyone calling at night. In the back garden a sunflood type of lamp with a halogen bulb of 500 watts (or even 300 watts) mounted high on the back wall about 40 feet (12 metres) from the ground should illuminate both the back of the house and an area of the garden of about 66 by 33 feet (20 by 10 metres). Remember that the aim of the sunflood at the back is to illuminate one side of the house and the escape route from it in the event of the alarm operating. An example of such a simple security lighting installation is shown in Figure 35.

If you have extensive grounds or dark corners or sheltering trees and shrubs near accessible doors and windows, then call in an expert and get his views on how you can eliminate these danger spots with sensible lighting. Incidentally, security lighting needs to be mounted out of reach of both vandals and the intending intruder.

Access Control

When someone rings the front-door bell of your house or flat, or the bell of a door-answering machine, you should always check who it is before opening the door, either through some viewing arrangement or by talking to them. If you don't recognize them, find out who they are and why they

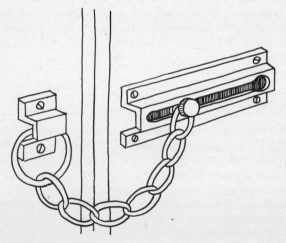

Figure 36. *Door chain*

have called. You may not wish to carry on such a discussion through a closed door, in which case put the door on its chain and then open it as far as it will go. Door chains of this type must be very firmly installed – in all too many instances the chain is far tougher than the wood to which it is fixed and a determined intruder can burst in (Figure 36). Remember that the door chain is not an additional bolt on the front door and should not be used as such, but as part of your access-control system; it should be able to withstand someone pushing against the door for sufficiently long for you to get to the telephone and call for help (or sound the alarm with your personal attack button).

If you decide to open the front door, don't let an unknown caller in unless it's absolutely necessary and they are authorized to do so. You should *always* check that they have the authority: a warrant card for a policeman, an identity card for meter readers, VAT men and so on. These individuals are required to identify themselves and have no rights of entry at all otherwise. Once they are in, close the front door and accompany your visitors to wherever they have to go, staying where you can keep an eye on them until you see them out of the front door again. If you talk to strangers in the living areas of the house be particularly careful of confidence tricksters, who come in all kinds of guises, but particularly as antique furniture dealers (with apologies to friends in that business).

When you move to a new house or flat you should always have the front- and probably the back-door lock changed. Make sure that you know who has copies of the new keys and don't let others have them without good reason. The same applies to keys for an alarm system, and as said before the keyholders must be thoroughly familiar with how to operate the alarm. So please don't be careless with your keys – *never* leave them under the front-door mat or on the lintel of the doorway, and if you lose them have the locks changed at once.

Cars

Cars are one of the biggest single items at risk. To have your car stolen can mean walking in the rain, not being able to do your work properly the next day or losing a substantial No Claims bonus on the insurance, so it's worth taking some steps to look after it.

Car thieves generally fall into three categories: the professional, who steals a particular car for resale either at home or abroad; the sneak thief, who is after the contents of the car such as an expensive coat, despatch case or even the car radio/cassette player; and lastly the joy-rider who needs to get home or to show off to his girlfriend or both. Each can usually get into a car and be away in a period of between thirty seconds and a minute. Cars have a number of security devices built in but they are too often not used by their owners. Arrangements in 1970, which required cars to have steering locks operated by the ignition key, would have made it slightly more difficult for thieves if car-owners could also be made to use the locks. At present, about eighty per cent of stolen cars are left with doors unlocked, and some twenty per cent with the ignition key in the car. So the first rule is to lock your car whenever you leave it unattended, and don't tempt the sneak thief by leaving attractive items exposed in the car – cover them with a rug or put them in the boot or in the locked glove compartment.

There are a number of ways of improving the security of your car at not too great a cost, and the following may be considered:

a. Additional locks on the doors (Figure 37a), boot and even special locks for the steering wheel (Krook Lock) or the gear lever;

b. Alarms, consisting of detectors, either as mechanical contacts on doors, bonnet and boot and/or vibration detectors which react to the car being tampered with or moved. These would include a control for switching the alarm on/off and signalling by bells, siren or the car's own horn (Figure 37b);

c. Immobilizers, which prevent the car from being run because they cut off the petrol-supply and the ignition. Obviously, the simplest way to immobilize the car yourself is to remove a vital part of the engine, such as the distributor arm;

d. Deterrents, which put the thief off attacking your particular car. One such system involves the etching of the car's registered number on the glass in the corner of each of the windows and the front and back windscreen. A thief would then not only have to change the registration plates and engine number, but replace all the windows as well. In other cases people put stickers on the car saying that it is protected by an alarm, but though this may occasionally work it is rather poor security.

As in other security situations, the physical strength provided by locks and bolts will delay the thief, but once inside the car he can adjust wires to start the engine, or take his time removing the radio or cutting the steering-wheel bolts. In fact, the easiest way to break into a locked car is to remove the rear window (with a screwdriver run around the rubber mounting it will come out in seconds). Consequently, an alarm system which only uses contacts on doors, boot and bonnet has its limitations. The vibration detector, which is set to react to high-frequency attacks such as those caused

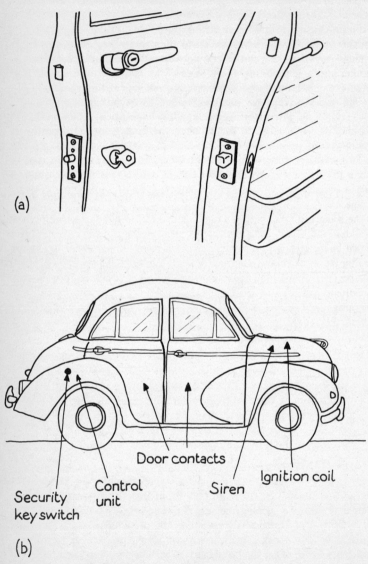

Figure 37. (a) *Additional locks on the doors* (b) *Car alarm layout*

by filing or levering metal or glass, but will not respond to the car being rocked by casual passers-by, is probably the best device to use, particularly if it has a separate siren for signalling (rather than using the car's horn). But care should be taken with the installation and setting of such an alarm to make sure that false alarms are not caused by passing vehicles or even another car 'touch-parking' in the street. The signal for a car should only operate for a short period, e.g. about half a minute, after which the controls should automatically re-set and continue guarding the car.

The technique of immobilizing a car, either by removing a part, or having a special device installed to cut off the petrol and ignition, is an effective way of preventing it from being driven off. But remember, if the car is one which professional thieves are likely to be interested in, they may push it into a low-loader vehicle or large van and take it bodily. Ownership of such a car carries with it the responsibility for keeping it in a secure garage.

The security of the garage should start with its physical protection. It should be of sound construction with an adequate roof and the doors should be well made with security locks on them, if necessary with a good locking bar and a high security padlock (Figure 38). The windows should also be well secured and locked, rather than just fastened. It is possible and often desirable to extend the alarm system you have in the house to the garage, and special heavy-duty contacts are available for garage doors (Figure 39).

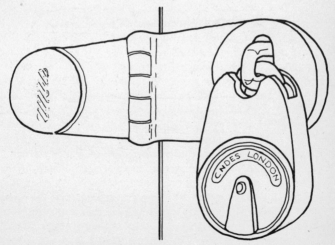

Figure 38. *High security padlock*

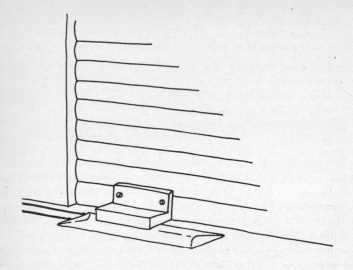

Figure 39. *Heavy duty magnetic contact for alarm of garage door*

During the holiday seasons many people carry goods on the roof rack of their car. Obviously these items are at risk if left unguarded. To lock them to the rack – and certain ski-racks have padlocks for the skis – is a step in the right direction only as long as it is not possible to unclip the whole rack from the car's guttering. A determined thief could transfer the lot on to his own car and take his time cutting through the shackles of the pad-locks in the peace of his own garage.

Other ideas for securing cars have been tried from time to time and though some appear attractive they have never been generally accepted on the market. For example, an ultrasonic detector inside a car should work well as it should only start the alarm when someone opened a door or window and got in the car. However, the relatively high cost of the unit has made it difficult to market. At the other extreme, there is available a bolt incorporating a lock and key with which you can secure the wheels of your car to prevent them from being stolen. To have your car stolen is both frustrating and expensive – the damage done may be in excess of the cost of replacement wheels and tyres.

Caravans

There are a number of ways in which a caravan is at risk:

a. It can be unhitched from your car and driven off on the back of someone else's;
b. It can be removed from its parking place at your home or on the campsite when you are not there;
c. It can be entered and equipment, as well as your personal effects, can be stolen.

To make sure that your caravan won't be unhitched from your car a special hitch lock is available, which has a simple key operation (Figure 40). This is, of course, also valuable as a safety device to prevent the accidental unhitching of your caravan over particularly bumpy country.

The simplest method of immobilizing a caravan is to remove its wheels and this is by far the best way of deterring anyone from removing it from your home. However, it is as well to keep the wheels indoors – or even just the wheel nuts – rather than in the caravan from which they can be removed, fitted and the whole taken off. At your campsite you may prefer

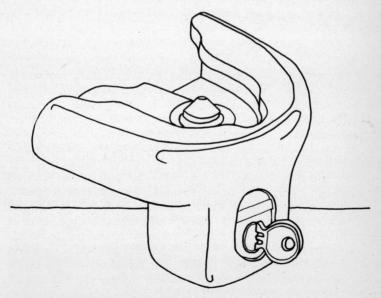

Figure 40. *Caravan hitchlock*

to use a device which can be clipped on the wheel and locked in position. This can also be applied when you stop temporarily (but remember to remove it before driving off!). Such a device can, of course, also be used for a horse box, boat trailer or glider trailer, and weighs about 4 lb (1.8 kg).

Because a caravan has to be of light weight it is comparatively easy to break into. However good the lock on the door, it will always be comparatively easy for a thief to force a window – or even the side panels. So the first thing to remember is never to leave valuable items in the caravan when it is unattended. It is, of course, possible to fit your caravan with a car-type alarm with its own battery, contacts on the door and windows and a signalling siren. This should incorporate a time switch to shut off the siren after about a minute and automatically reset the alarm. Again, the use of an ultrasonic detector inside the caravan would be an effective solution if you were prepared to pay its comparatively high price.

A recent case of theft from a caravan involved a couple travelling through Italy towards the East. During the night, a window was removed while they were asleep, a gas spray was introduced to ensure that they slept more soundly, and all their money, passports, travellers cheques and other valuables like watches were stolen. The next morning they awoke rather late and sleepy, and then had to spend the next week with consuls and banks, acquiring the documents and money they needed to get anywhere. So do keep travel documents and the bulk of your money in a very secure and secret place in the vehicle. For a long trip like the one described, it would have been worth having a wall safe, with a combination lock (so that there is no key to worry about when you are swimming), welded into the vehicle at the start.

Motorcycles

Thousands of motorcycles are stolen or vandalized every year and the insurance compensation is seldom adequate, while the next premium is likely to be prohibitive. As in the case of steering locks for cars, the fork lock on a motorcycle is helpful, but can be overcome or broken by the casual thief – while the professional will probably load the whole thing into his van.

To achieve better physical security, attach the motorcycle, with a substantial lock and chain passed through the frame and at least the front wheel, to an immovable object like a lamp post – or a tree. This means using a fairly long chain, so be careful not to put it round an object like a parking meter, with enough slack for the chain to be lifted over the meter.

A number of alarms are available for motorcycles which use a vibration detector to indicate the machine is being interfered with, or a mercury switch to detect that it is being lifted or pushed. Such alarms need to have their own battery power supply, as the accumulator of a motorcycle is usually very easy to get at and disconnect.

The use of an immobilizer, which will cut off the ignition and the petrol supply on a motorcycle, is effective as long as it can be sufficiently hidden from view.

Bicycles

If you have bought a bicycle recently you will know why they are such attractive targets to thieves. In a major city, you can be certain of losing your cycle within days if it is not very substantially locked and chained whenever you leave it unattended. The ease with which a bicycle thief can use bolt croppers to cut steel wire, light chains or the shackles of poor padlocks has to be seen to be appreciated.

The only solution is to obtain a really heavy strong chain and then spend a bit of money on a security padlock which will stand up to attack – for a good time at least. After that, always make sure that you pass the chain through the back wheel and the frame and attach it to something immovable. Again, beware of parking meters, as the whole bicycle can very often be lifted off and taken away, unless it is very tightly attached.

A final point is that you should always make sure you know the serial number, or numbers, of your cycle. If it does get stolen you will need to tell the police its make, type and number, so make a note of these as soon as you get the machine.

Boats

Boats, whether yachts, cruisers, speedboats or dinghies, are particularly vulnerable to criminals because they have a high value in themselves, often have expensive equipment on them, and are left unattended for long periods. If they are moored it is easy to approach them unobserved by dinghy and they are easily broken into. They usually contain radios, navigation equipment, TVs, binoculars, tape gear and probably an outboard motor.

The physical protection of boats is not easy, but they can be made more difficult to steal by using an immobilizer on the fuel system, or by removing the sails, the outboard motor or the oars. The outboard itself can be secured by a special lock applied to the clamping screws to prevent them from being loosened off without the key of the lock cylinder (Figure 41).

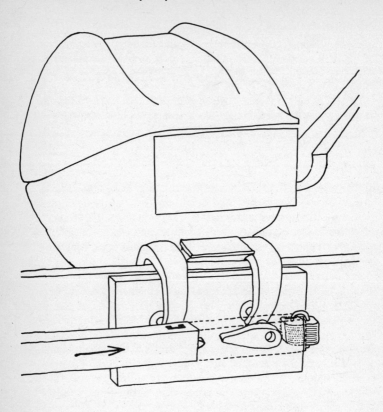

Figure 41. *Lock for an outboard motor*

On yachts and cruisers the use of alarms is probably the better security solution, though all such equipment would have to be fully weatherproofed. The detectors would normally be either magnetic contacts on all hatches, ports, windows or doors; or vibration sensors around the hull and cabin, carefully set to distinguish between attacks on the craft and its rocking or rubbing against a mooring; or an ultrasonic detector in the main cabin, which would react to any movement in that space. In each case the alarm would have a control unit for testing and setting and would be operated off the boat's main batteries, but also have an emergency standby battery

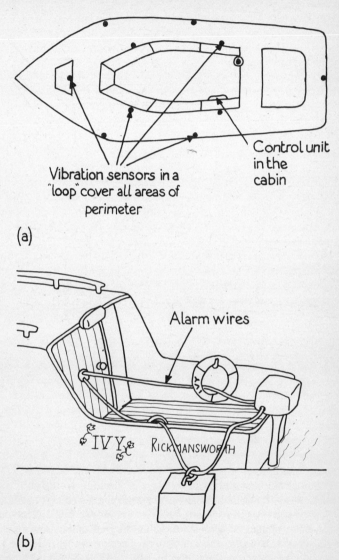

(a)

Vibration sensors in a "loop" cover all areas of perimeter

Control unit in the cabin

Alarm wires

(b)

Figure 42. (a) *Alarm layout for a boat* (b) *Use of a closed circuit loop*

of its own (Figure 42a). The signalling device would probably be a klaxon or siren, associated with a flashing lamp, though where there is a telephone connection to the shore, a '999' automatic dialling system could also be used. The enormous capital cost of some yachts would clearly make it worth installing as sophisticated a system as one has in a house.

Another advantage of having an alarm on the boat is that it can be connected, by means of the closed-circuit wiring, to items like the outboard motor on the dinghy and a loop can even be passed through a mooring ring (Figure 42b). Other points worth considering for improving the security of your boat are as follows:

a. Painting on the name of the boat and any other identification is better than screwing it on or using adhesive lettering: it will take several coats of paint to obliterate the original painted name;
b. Engrave a registered number on all removable valuable items of equipment in the boat, such as compasses, beacons, depth finders, winches and the outboard, so that they can be positively identified and recovered;
c. Do not leave any registration papers aboard the boat when you leave it unattended;
d. Using one-way screws to fix down bolted or screwed-down equipment deters the thief from taking such things.

Miscellaneous

A general point to remember is that you should be careful not to provide a burglar with the tools for carrying out a robbery. Leaving hammers, large screwdrivers, spanners and, especially, ladders in a garden shed or the garage is subjecting the opportunist to too much temptation – and he is the most likely of all burglars. It is worth checking from time to time what is kept in these places to make sure nothing could be misused.

The villain also misuses information, so don't make it obvious when you are going to be away and don't tell people in general about valuable possessions.

Finally, please remember that the success of all your security measures will be a 'non-event' – that is, the fact that no disaster has struck means that the precautions you have taken and your attitude to security have kept you clear of trouble.

Check List

1. Do you check that you know a person before opening the front door to them – always?
2. Who else has keys to your front door and do you know they look after these keys as carefully as you do?
3. When you go on holiday, do you stop the paper and milk and do you tell the police you will be away?
4. Are visitors to your front door properly illuminated at night, so that you really can identify them? Have you thought of using floodlights in the garden and do you know how inexpensive they are?
5. Do you always check the credentials of meter readers and are you prepared to firmly not open the front door to a salesman (or carol singer)?
6. Do you always lock your car when you leave it and have you thought of installing additional security devices?
7. If you have a caravan or boat, do you take precautions to ensure that neither it nor any equipment gets stolen?
8. Do you know the serial number and type of bicycle you or your children have? Does it have a substantial chain and proper padlock on it?
9. Is the garage for your car properly secured and are there any tools there which could be used by a burglar to get into the house? Where do you keep your ladder?
10. Do you tell everyone at the local pub when you are going away on holiday and do you tell them all about your caravan/boat/cottage in the country? There may well be a greedy villain listening too!

Chapter 7
Fire

7. Fire

The Danger

Fire regulations are an area of security widely covered by legislation in the case of public premises, but it is left to the individual to take the necessary precautions in his own home, caravan or boat, where the dangers are still very real. Every year nearly a thousand people in the United Kingdom (mainly those over 65 or under 16) die as a result of fire in their own homes.

People have become so accustomed to making use of fire that they are often not sufficiently aware of the potential danger of ordinary household items. Matches are of course the most obvious example: children will incorporate the behaviour of their parents into their games and will almost certainly light matches if they can get hold of a box. This is the direct cause of nearly half of all domestic fires.

In financial terms the costs of a major fire are enormous and to lose your possessions is extremely traumatic – in many ways more devastating than a burglary because fire, unlike a burglar, is unselective, and may leave nothing at all.

However, the most serious aspect of domestic fires is the possible loss of life. A smouldering fire started by a carelessly dropped cigarette may take about three hours to build up, all the while giving off fumes. At first the fumes are slight and a sleeping family may grow accustomed to them and die in their sleep before the build-up of fumes finally 'flashes over' and flames engulf the house. How much time a family would have to escape at this point would depend on their house and how combustible the furniture and fittings were, but above all on whether or not they had shut their bedroom doors and knew what to do in the emergency.

As in other security situations it is important to have a balanced view of the threat and how to live with it. Fortunately, the steps which should be taken to reduce the risk of fire are generally very straightforward and, since the consequence of fire may be death, well worth the costs involved.

Causes and Prevention

Most fires are started through ignorance or carelessness. Listed in order of frequency, the main causes of fire in the home are as follows:

a. Matches, in the hands of children;
b. Cookers, particularly with deep frying;
c. Electric appliances, such as radiant fires and blankets;
d. Unguarded, unswept chimneys, open fires and paraffin heaters;
e. Careless disposal of cigarettes and matches by adults (particularly the aged and infirm);
f. Electric wiring, left unrepaired and frayed, or overloaded or unsuitably run;
g. Inflammable materials or tools kept (often under the stairs) and used in the home for do-it-yourself or other purposes;
h. Arson, criminal damage.

Small children should of course never be left in the house on their own. Not only are they liable to find and play with matches, but there are innumerable other ways in which they can start fires in the course of their games. A tragically high proportion of fire casualities are children, not only because they are less able to escape, but also because they so often start fires when left on their own (it is after all something they are encouraged to enjoy on 5 November). It is obviously asking for trouble to leave a child in a room where there is an open fire – the fire should always have an adequate guard in front of it whenever the child is playing in the room, whether alone or not.

Most people have experienced a fire with the cooker. The majority are small and, though potentially dangerous, are generally easily smothered. But with a slightly larger fire – say with deep-frying fat alight – the dangers mount up at an alarming rate. It only requires someone to hurl a bucket of water at the blaze or to try to carry the pan out of the kitchen and drop it for the whole place to go up in flames in seconds. So cooker fires should always be treated seriously and lessons learned from the experience so that it does not have to be repeated or extended. As a general rule cooker fires should be smothered, either with a proper cloth or with a metal cover for the pan – and the gas or electricity cut off at once.

Electric appliances, such as radiant fires, electric blankets, toasters in which the bread jams and gets dug out with a knife, free-standing and movable cooker rings, are all potential fire starters. In fact, wherever you have an electric heater element exposed, great care should be taken with it. Where the element is not exposed there is the danger that it might be left on and forgotten when standing on inflammable material – the electric iron left on the board while you answer the telephone is a classic case.

People often expose themselves to the risk of fire through meanness. You may have got used to the foibles of your old electric fire, with its botched-up, squiggly element, but have you considered that new equipment would give you additional heat and use less electricity? 'Making do' with electric appliances is seldom good economics and nearly always dangerous. Another way in which electric appliances can start fires is if too many are connected to one socket, so overloading a circuit. Christmas, too, is a time of additional risk if electric lights are used for the tree without due care. Obviously an electrical short can start a far too merry blaze in a dry fir tree.

Electric blankets are a particular hazard because they are close to your body for so long. Not only should they carry the British Standards sign, but they must be used the way the manufacturer says. Underblankets should not be used on top and none should be left on all night unless the instructions say that this is all right. Finally, they should be properly serviced every two years. Do not fold them as this can break wires inside.

Open fires are obvious points from which household fires can start. If the chimney is not regularly swept, the soot up the chimney will eventually catch and cause a fire, the extent of which will only be limited by the quality of the chimney and how well it has been looked after over the years. A spark from an open fire can easily set furniture, carpet or curtains alight, so it needs to be supervised very carefully and again the best solution is the use of a fireguard properly secured to the wall. These should carry the 'kitemark' of the British Standards Institute: bs 2788 is the appropriate one in this case. Fireplaces themselves get old in time and after faithful service may well start cracking up. If they do, these cracks are routes for embers to filter through and set light to wooden joists or other timbers beyond. Modern paraffin and calor gas fires have been made very much safer than they used to be, partly as a result of the efforts of the British Standards Institute. The main risks with these are that paraffin heaters may get knocked over, while a gas fire is likely to draw to it any lightweight garments in its vicinity and set them alight.

Carelessness with electric irons has already been mentioned, but a far more prevalent cause of fires is the carelessness of some smokers. Because smoking is a habit, many of the 'rituals' associated with it – lighting the match and flicking it away, knocking out a pipe in preparation for a meal, stubbing a cigarette inadequately or just throwing it into a waste-paper basket – are carried out without thinking. If a fire does start as a result, the smoker has often long since gone elsewhere and would never dream that he had been the cause of a particular tragedy. A smouldering fire is frequently caused by a cigarette falling into a settee or easy chair – or even by an ashtray with glowing ends slipping off the arm of a chair – and not being noticed when people go to bed. Always check under cushions last thing at night.

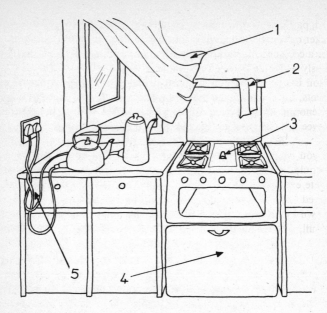

Figure 43. *Danger points in the kitchen – can you see why?*

Electric wiring itself has often been installed in a house many years before its present occupants moved in. However good it was in the first place, it is bound to deteriorate in time. In many houses built or rewired before 1950 an old type of cotton-covered flex with rubber insulation was used. Such wiring is bound to be suspect after over thirty years: the insulation will have rotted and there will be a considerable loss of electricity even when all the appliances are turned off; it should be checked every 5 years. It is far too easy to overload such a system and when a major short does take place the heat generated in the wiring will start a fire without any kind of warning – except the chaotic darkness caused by fuses blowing.

These days more and more people are doing their own decorating and other jobs around the house and many of the tools and materials used are fire hazards. The professional is taught the safety rules which apply to each, but the amateur does not get this training; nor does he often take much notice of warnings on products such as tins containing adhesives, telling him to keep doors and windows open because of the inflammable vapours given off. The amateur blow-lamp user can be a very obvious hazard, particularly if he tries to mend pipes below the floorboards without a bucket of water handy, while the general distribution of soldering irons can be a considerable hazard if they do not have proper stands and are left carelessly while the latest electronic circuitry is perfected.

Arson is one of the most frequent causes of fires in commercial establishments, but fairly uncommon in private houses, and unless you are unlucky enough to live beside offices from which a vicious and disgruntled employee has been sacked, the risk from this cause is small.

Once you become aware of the danger of fire and how it can be caused you should be able to recognize risk areas in your home. Figures 43 and 44 illustrate examples of very obvious risks. You may feel that these are too contrived – but then have a critical look at your own house and check on your own habits. And we've left out the spare can of paraffin, kept in the back hall, which adds up to a whole series of risks on its own account.

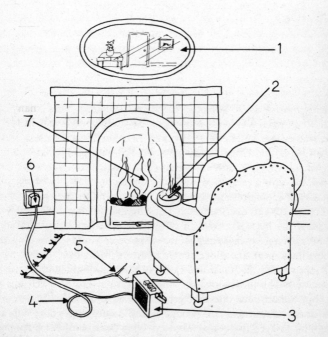

Figure 44. *Can you see the dangers in the siting room?*

Means of Escape

As was made clear in Chapter 5 the two first and most important steps in
a security situation are:

a. Avoidance or prevention – in this case, take all reasonable steps to
   ensure that a fire doesn't start;
b. Escape – if a fire does start, then you and your family have got to be
   able to get out of the house.

Once a fire has started in a particular room it will tend to spread through
the main communicating areas of the house. If there are stairs it will almost
certainly spread up them, and as they are usually made of wood and
carpeted, the speed with which it travels and increases in intensity is fright-
ening – a matter of seconds. If there are no stairs, then passageways offer a
clear route for draught to feed oxygen to the fire and for it to spread
quickly. Any closed door obviously checks the fire from penetrating for a
time, depending on what the door is made of and above all how substantial
it is. Consequently you should get into the habit of keeping doors shut
whenever possible. If you need to go through a doorway after a fire has
started, always feel the door before you open it to make sure that it is
not hot with the fire blazing on the other side. If it is hot, then you have
just got to find another way out, because to open the door could be
fatal.

In considering how you would escape from a fire, begin by shutting off
the stairs, or the main passageway if there are no stairs. Now how do you
get out? If yours is a terraced house could you climb on to the roof from
the top-floor rooms and get down via your neighbour's house? If you
think so, try it. Maybe you think you could make the bed sheets into a
rope: just try it and see what you would tie the end to (the bed leg?) and
what it's like getting down that way. If you are not prepared to get down
like that, then you should have some sort of collapsible ladder in the room
for use in an emergency (see Figure 45). Again, don't wait for the crisis to
find it won't fit or reach, but try it out calmly to give yourself confidence
and then get your family to test it.

It's worth remembering that if there's no safer alternative it's possible to
jump from a height of 15–20 feet (4½–6 metres) without damage, and that
you can decrease the distance by at least 6 feet by letting yourself down to
arms' length before dropping (see Figure 46). As every parachutist will tell
you, keep your legs together, knees slightly bent, and roll over as you land.

Once you have worked out a plan of escape, make sure that everyone in
the house knows and understands it. This will give them both an awareness

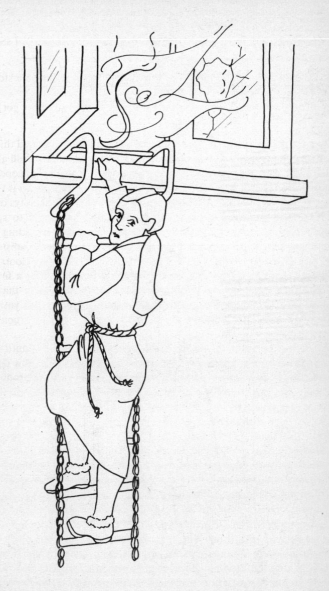

Figure 45. *A simple escape ladder*

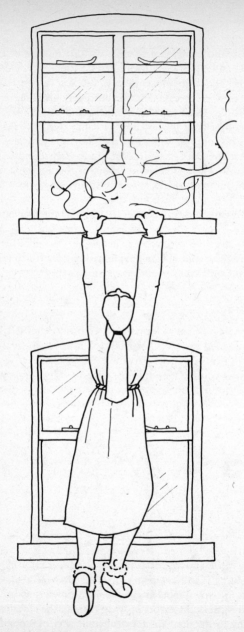

Figure 46. *Halving the distance to drop*

of the fire risk and confidence to cope with it. Beware of the quality of escape devices and check them with our Fire Prevention Officer.

A final word about fire precautions in relation to physical defences: as you develop your defences against an intruder, installing bars, grilles or particularly strong locks on both windows and doors, give a thought to how you would get out in the event of a fire. Usually, the answer is to leave door keys on the wall opposite the doors, where they cannot be reached from outside – even through the cat flap – and to keep keys for window grilles in a safe place in the room. Never fix the key to the grille itself or to the knob of the door. Glazing fails quickly in a fire; Georgian wired glazing lasts about 30 minutes.

Fire defence and physical defences may seem at cross purposes, and the plans often work out that way if the two problems (and the experts offering solutions) are dealt with completely separately. So consider both at the same time and there should be no incompatibility; if for some reason there is, always make the priority your means of escape.

Fire-Fighting

The essential thing to remember is that you must *always* call for help from the Fire Service (see pp. 126–7), unless you are able to extinguish the fire immediately (if it is in a waste paper bin, for instance). If you do propose to tackle the fire yourself, get everyone else out of the house first.

Fires are caused by combining heat, oxygen and fuel, so the basic princi-

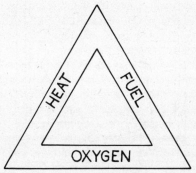

ple of fire-fighting is to remove one of these three elements. If someone's clothes catch fire you should make them lie down (and so protect their face) and roll them in the carpet or wrap them in the curtains – to prevent oxygen getting to the fire. The most obvious way of stopping a fire in a wastepaper basket is to empty a pail of water over it, thus immediately reducing the temperature. If, however, you did the same thing when you saw a frayed bit of wiring to an electric heater start smouldering in the carpet you would be in a lot of trouble: although the smouldering might be doused, you would probably short all the electrics in the house and even give yourself a severe shock. Equally, putting water on to a deep-fry fire could be disastrous because water falling into boiling fat forms steam bubbles which explode and may shoot the burning liquid all over the kitchen – injuring you and setting the whole kitchen alight. So clearly it's vital to know which method of fire-fighting to use.

The main fire-fighting weapons available for the home are as follows:

a. Water in a bucket or in a red-coloured fire extinguisher;
b. Smothering blanket in a special container from which it can be pulled out easily, ready for immediate use;
c. Vapouring liquid (BCF)* in a green extinguisher: for fires caused by electricity or burning liquids;
d. Carbon dioxide (CO_2) in a black extinguisher which delivers a powerful concentration of the gas through a special funnel (which also helps to distinguish it): for most kinds of fire;
e. Foam in a cream-coloured extinguisher: for liquids on fire;
f. Dry powder in a black extinguisher: for most kinds of fire.

Even if you had all the extinguishers around, you would never remember which extinguisher to use in a particular crisis. What you need is something which will be effective immediately to hand. It should also be noted that foam and dry powder extinguishers, though very effective, leave an appalling mess and can damage furnishings extensively. Carbon Dioxide is very good and versatile, but must not be used in a confined space with people present, and many people may hesitate at the price.

This leaves the first three weapons mentioned. In most houses water is readily available and as long as there are adequate containers (a tooth mug will not help much), the red extinguishers are probably unnecessary. In the kitchen, you should keep a smother blanket in a place from which it can be easily snatched in an emergency – *not* buried at the back of the broom cupboard nor in a drawer. Elsewhere in the house, there should also be a general-purpose extinguisher, probably the vapouring liquid type. Remember to mount the extinguisher well away from where you expect the fire to take place – not right beside the cooker for instance – or you will be unable to get at it just when it is most needed. Also, be very careful to have extinguishers regularly serviced, with the dates on which this was

* Bromochlorodifluoromethane.

Figure 47. *Using a smother blanket*

done marked on them. Make sure they are fully charged and BSS/FOC approved. Do *not* use small aerosols.

If you have a large home, or even if you are worried about what you

Figure 48. *How to use an extinguisher*

should do in a more modest one, contact the Fire Prevention Officer of your local Fire Brigade and ask for his advice – he gives it free, as do the suppliers of commmercial equipment. His telephone number is in the directory.

Calling for Help

On discovering a fire the first thing to do is to call for help. Shout out of a window, operate the intruder alarm and dial '999' on the telephone. There is no charge and your insurance claim may be affected if there is a delay. When the voice from the Post Office Exchange asks 'Which emergency service?' just say 'Fire' firmly and you will be put through to the Fire Brigade Headquarters. Their essential requirement is to know where the fire is, so that they can get someone moving at once. Once they have got this information they may well go on to ask further details, but it's vital that you should first clearly tell them your full address and telephone number. The Fire Service keep recordings of all calls and the really tragic ones are from people who in a panic just shout down the telephone for help and will not listen to the operator's persistent question of 'Where?' In fact the operator will always try to have the call traced during such an exchange, but this is bound to waste valuable minutes.

So make sure that everyone in the house, children included, know that if there is a fire they should dial '999', ask for 'Fire', and tell the Fire Service *where* the fire is.

Fire Alarms

The principles of fire alarms are very similar to those of intruder alarms with detectors, controls and signalling all incorporated in the system. There are two basic types of fire detectors:

a. Smoke detector, and
b. Heat detector.

Again, smoke detectors come in two sorts: those which are designed to detect smoke by means of a photoelectric cell, and others operating on the principle of an ionization chamber, which react to both smoke and fumes. In the case of the photoelectric-cell type (Figure 49a), smoke entering the tube will obscure the pilot lamp from the cell and so initiate the alarm. With the other type a very small amount of radioactive substance is used to ionize the air around the sensor. The ionized air conducts electricity very slightly but smoke and fumes reduce this conductivity and the sensor reacts by initiating the alarm.

Heat detectors are used in various forms. The most simple should normally be found on the oil fuel supply of a central heating boiler. This is a soft metal link which will melt if the temperature rises over a certain limit, and in the case of a boiler it would be connected to a shut-off valve to stop the oil flow if the metal melted. Others are designed to measure a rapid rise in temperature. These contain a bi-metal lever, which distorts when the temperature changes quickly because one metal expands more rapidly than the other (Figure 49b). Again when this occurs the alarm is started.

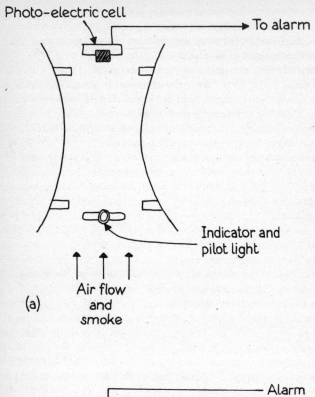

Photo-electric cell

To alarm

Indicator and
pilot light

Air flow
and
smoke

(a)

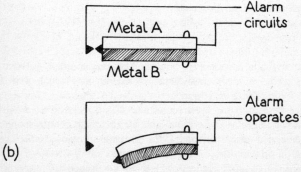

Metal A

Metal B

Alarm
circuits

Alarm
operates

(b)

Figure 49. (a) *Photo-electric cell smoke detector* (b) *Rapid heat-rise detector*

The control for a fire alarm provides power, standby batteries and the means of testing the system and switching it on and off. The layout will usually include a number of circuits relating to various parts of the house or the different types of detectors used. There should usually be a 'break glass' detector on the system and this operates in the same way as the personal attack button on the intruder alarm. It allows anyone who discovers a fire in the house to sound the alarm directly, without waiting for detectors to do their automatic work.

The local signalling can consist of bells, sirens or even hooters and the system can include automatic signalling through the '999' service or on a direct line to the Fire Service or central station of a security company.

In the design of the system it is usually best to use heat detectors in the kitchen, garage or where the central-heating boiler is, and smoke detectors on landings or above the stairs or in passages where fumes might make their poisonous way. The controls and signalling unit can be put out of the way as they do not have to be switched on and off regularly – they are always left on, except when you test them to make sure they are working properly. Fire alarms should always be installed by professionals because the wiring must be protected against fire. It is normally run in metal-cased wire or through metal tubing (conduit).

For a small house, there are a number of self-contained smoke detectors available. These usually operate on the ionization chamber principle, are battery powered and have their own horn to signal with. They usually incorporate a testing button and an indicator to show when the battery is losing its power. If you can't afford a full alarm system, it would be a sensible measure to install a small unit of this kind on the ceiling of the landing outside your bedroom.

Fire Resistant Materials

Since a fire may destroy everything you possess you may well feel that it is worth while having a fire-resistant container into which you could put Wills, Deeds, Birth and Marriage Certificates, Passport, Tax Records, Insurance Policies, Share Certificates and so on. Deposit boxes, such as the one shown in Figure 50, are available for this purpose at reasonable cost – but remember that such boxes are not safes. Equally, safes used in the home will provide little or no fire resistance.

There are certain chemicals which can be applied to materials to make them fire resistant or flame proof. These range from diammonium phosphate for various fabrics, to borax and boric acid for fabrics, paper and cardboard. Always use proper lighting sets (BSS) on Christmas trees.

Figure 50. *Deposit box*

British Standards Institute

The British Standards mentioned are as follows:

BS 2788 – Fire guards for open fires
BS 3300 – Oil heaters
BS 3456 – All electrical appliances
BS 5258 – Gas fires

Check List

1. Have you had a fire in your house? What have you done to prevent it ever happening again?
2. What means have you of knowing that a fire has started – in the night?
3. What would you do first on discovering a fire in your house?
4. Have you anything with which to fight a fire – on the cooker? – if the sitting-room furniture were alight?

5. How will you and your family escape if there is a fire on the stairs in the night? Do the others know?

6. How will you call the Fire Service and how long do you think they will take to get to you?

7. If you are trapped in a room when there is a fire what will you do?

8. Are you fully covered for fire in your insurance? Is the value you have given your house and contents realistic?

9. When was your house wired and have you had it checked by an electrician since?

10. Have you used a fire extinguisher and do you know how to?

Chapter 8
The Protectors

8. The Protectors

The Police

The action of the police in responding to calls for help has already been mentioned. It is, however, important to understand why they should respond in this way to such a call, what they can do when they come, and to realize that in certain cases they can do nothing – or no more than any other citizen. For instance, if the police are called to intervene in a brawl which turns out to be a domestic argument they will be at pains to calm the whole situation down, so that other people are not inconvenienced by it, but thereafter it is up to the two antagonists to sort out their differences – peaceably. At the other end of the scale, for example a hostage-taking situation, the police may decide that they can no longer handle the situation and will hand over the responsibility to the military authorities, as in the siege of the Iranian Embassy in London in 1980. In this case the authority of the Home Secretary had to be obtained before the formal handover of powers could take place.

History. It is perhaps important to know something of how we came to have a police force before considering the powers we give to it – if any. When the Anglo-Saxons took over the country, after the Romans left, they brought with them a system of collective pledging, which meant that the headman and members of each settlement were responsible for the internal peace of the locality. Every ten families were gathered into a group in which all the adult males formed a tything, lead by a tythingman. Should any member of the group commit a crime, the others were responsible for producing him for trial. If they failed to do this, the group had to pay compensation. Groups of ten tythings were formed in a hundred, the head of which was a hundredman, who exercised administrative and judicial power through the court of the hundred. Placed above the hundredman was the shire-reeve or sheriff, who was responsible to the king for keeping the peace in the shire. If necessary, he could summon a sheriff's 'posse', or anyone in the community could be called on to join in pursuing a felon when a 'hue and cry' was raised. In this way the king was able to maintain 'the king's peace'.

When the Normans came in 1066 they maintained the system and called the collective responsibility of the community the 'frankpledge'. As towns grew in size and population, order was kept by 'watch and word', whereby the gates were closed at sunset and watchmen posted. London, in addition, had a 'marching watch' or mobile patrol system. All of this seems remarkably familiar.

The term 'constable' came into use in about 1240 and the tythingman became the petty or parish constable with responsibilities for:

– Supervising the watchmen;
– Inquiring into offences;
– Serving summonses;
– Executing warrants;
– Taking charge of prisoners;
– Organizing the 'hue and cry'.

In the next century the knights appointed to keep the peace were replaced by justices (hence Justice of the Peace), who were local landowners, men of position and authority in the locality, with the constable answering to them. The structure for maintaining the peace is the same today, as is the collective responsibility of everyone in the community to keep it that way.

With the dramatic improvements in communications and the mobility of people in the eighteenth century, the unpaid constables were unable to maintain law and order. Their task became so difficult or dangerous that they appointed substitutes and paid them a small wage to do the job. The night watchmen were also appointed by the municipal authorities and those in London, started at the time of Charles II, were known as 'Charlies'. However, both the substitute constables and charlies became demoralized – often drunk or so incapable that they did little to suppress crime, if indeed they were not a part of it. As crime grew, punishments were made increasingly savage, but seemed to be no deterrent.

In the middle of the century new ideas began to circulate and Henry Fielding, the Chief Magistrate at Bow Street, did much to publicize the corruptness of justice in London and the level of unpunished crime. He was responsible first for the establishment of the Bow Street Foot and Horse Patrol, a body of full-time, uniformed patrols, and then of the Bow Street Runners whose task was to detect and apprehend criminals.

A force of full-time professional police was set up in Dublin in 1786 – the first time the word 'police' had been used – and in 1792 a number of Police Offices, as the magistrates' courts were called, were set up in Middlesex. A few years later a police force was set up for the Port of London and this was officially recognized as the Thames River Police Force in

1800. Progress continued to be slow and it was not until almost thirty years later that Sir Robert Peel was instrumental in the formation of the Metropolitan Police Force, known because of him as 'bobbies'. They had responsibility for policing the same area as the Bow Street patrols, which was a seven-mile radius from Charing Cross, but did not include the City of London, which later formed its own force. In the towns of England and Wales police forces were established under an Act of 1835, while the County Police Act of 1839 allowed the justices in the counties to establish their own full-time paid forces – though some counties did not trouble to set up forces for some time because the incidence of crime was so low in country areas.

Function. When the Metropolitan Police was formed its policy was stated to be as follows: 'The primary object of an efficient Police force is the prevention of crime: the next, that of detection and punishment of offenders if crime is committed.'

Its function has not been altered, though its powers and techniques have been changed by various Acts of Parliament and local authorities. The Metropolitan Police have always been under the ultimate control of the Home Secretary, while other forces are answerable to local bodies (who recognize the function of their police to be the same as that set out for the Metropolitan Police).

The collective power of citizens still exists, but the police are given certain additional powers to carry out their task – just as members of the armed services are. The issue of a Warrant to a policeman is his authority for the exercise of those extra powers. For instance, all citizens may arrest any person who has committed theft, but in doing so they must be certain that he has committed that crime. Police, on the other hand, can arrest a person if they have reasonable grounds for thinking that a theft was committed.

The Fire Service

History. Organized fire-fighting in London started as a direct result of the Great Fire of 1666. A number of insurance companies formed their own separate brigades to tackle fires and salvage goods at premises insured by them. By 1833 the majority of these London companies found it best to pool their fire-fighting resources and the London Fire Engine Establishment was set up and maintained by them. It was led by a professional fire-fighter from Edinburgh – James Braidwood. His tragic death and the high cost of insurance claims following a major conflagration in 1861 alerted the public and the Government to the fact that London's fire protection was too big a job for this small private brigade. Accordingly the Metropolitan Fire Brigade came into being on 1 January 1866 – paid for from public funds. This was led by Braidwood's successor, Captain Eyre Massey Shaw, who developed the Brigade, made wide use of steam fire-engines, telegraph systems and street fire-escape stations and initiated fire inspections of public buildings. The London County Council was formed in 1889 and took over the Brigade. The fire services were nationalized during the Second World War but returned to local authority control in 1948. Under the re-organization of London government, the Greater London Council was formed in 1965. This was the new fire authority, and nine brigades were wholly or partly merged to form the present brigade. In a similar way brigades were formed both in towns and country areas, with responsibility for their actions resting with the local authorities.

Function. The fire services are highly organized and well equipped to help those in trouble with fire. Firemen say that people often delay calling the fire brigade because they think the fire is too small to bother them with, or because they think someone else may already have called the brigade. So remember, if you see a fire, however small, don't hesitate to call the fire brigade immediately: you may save a life.

Insurance

History. The business of insurance has been conducted throughout history, with the earliest reference to life insurance going back to Babylonian tablets of 2123 BC in King Hammurabbi's time. The ships from Rhodes in 349 BC had 'cover', but the insurance lender was required to travel on board, while the Roman statesman Cato was reported to have lent money on ships in AD 149.

In this country, Queen Elizabeth's Privy Council, with the Lord Mayor of London, set up a form of insurance in the Royal Exchange in 1601. This was followed by Francis Bacon's Act of Parliament establishing the Court of Assurance. At Edward Lloyd's Coffee House, merchants, ships' captains and owners met in 1680 and started the present-day system of marine assurance.

In 1833 the fire brigades belonging to insurance companies were amalgamated to form the London Fire Engine Establishment, and industrial insurance was also started. The first insurance on rail travel was offered in 1845, and in 1914 the first cover for damage due to enemy aircraft.

Function. Insurance is provided to give people a means of protecting themselves against the financial losses of unexpected events. Its function therefore is the provision of financial security to its customers.

The way in which it works is through a contract. You pay an agreed amount, the premium, to the insurer, who undertakes to pay you a sum of money in the event of a particular circumstance. You can insure for almost anything – good weather on the occasion of the charity cricket match or against having twins – but make sure that you are not going to pay more in premiums than the cost of the possible loss you are insuring against – and remember that it is a financial loss, rather than an emotional one.

To enter into this contract you fill in a proposal form from the insurer, who asks you a large number of questions about yourself and your circumstances, as well as about what is to be insured. The information you provide will form the basis of the contract which is drawn up and so must be accurate and kept up to date, or the contract may not be valid. To discover this at the time you need to make a claim is far too late.

The insurer can, of course, decide not to enter into a contract at all because of what you have said on your proposal form. In some cases, the insurers recognize the large risks involved and raise the premium accordingly. For example the premium for insuring a senior executive travelling to certain parts of South America is likely to be very high indeed.

Making a Claim. Friends I have in insurance always emphasize the advantage of reporting losses to the police and keeping a record of the steps you take in making a claim. In claiming on your insurer you are asking him to keep his side of the contract by reimbursing you for a financial loss you have suffered. The way in which you should go about it is as follows:

a. Make sure that the contract covers this particular loss, i.e. look at the insurance policy itself and make certain you are covered;
b. Tell the insurer as quickly as possible that you wish to claim on the insurance. Many policies have a time limit for making a claim;
c. The insurer will then, almost certainly, send you a claim form. Answer this truthfully and accurately – remember that insurance companies have been in business for a very long time and most frauds have been tried before (often!). Return the claim form, with any estimates of cost of repairs or original bills you may be asked for, as well as details of when and to whom in the police you reported a loss;
d. The insurer may discuss the claim with you for a number of reasons, usually to do with the terms of the contract. If there are any doubts about the claim he may ask an assessor to look into the case further. In extreme cases, the claim may be taken to arbitration or even to

court. Remember that it is up to you, the policy holder, to prove that the loss occurred, which is why keeping records is so important;

e. The claim is settled by the insurer sending you a cheque. In practice most insurance companies are good at paying out on claims, not only when they are clearly within the terms of the policy, but also border-line cases. Most claims of up to about £50 are paid without any argument;

f. Finally, remember that after a claim the total sum insured is reduced by the amount paid out, until you have replaced and reinsured the item lost.

This may all seem obvious but most cases of theft and fire cause considerable emotional stress and people may not remember to take the simple steps necessary to cover their insurance requirements. You should check your insurance policy at regular intervals, not only to make sure you still have it, but to see that it covers your changing circumstances. The kind of questions to ask yourself and then check with the policy are:

a. Is the cost of rebuilding my house going to be covered by the sum insured?

b. Does the policy cover the contents, including the property of everyone in the house and the hired TV set?

c. Does the fire policy cover all eventualities except war, including arson?

d. Is flood damage covered and does the policy holder have to pay the first £15?

e. What happens if the house is sublet or part of it is sublet? Will the policy cover this situation?

f. If there was a major theft, could you really remember what was in the house?

g. Are there any warranties with the policy, such as the requirement to use a burglar alarm if the house is left unoccupied for more than six hours?

Commercial Security

Once more there is nothing new about commercial security. The use of mercenaries goes back into history, while the development of the police from the sub-contract hiring of constables in the eighteenth century has already been mentioned. However, the enormous rate of growth of the commercial security industry in the latter half of this century has been remarkable.

Clearly, the increase in crime and the ability or otherwise of society to cope with it has established the need for additional security services. While the capabilities of the police and fire services have been greatly increased with new equipment and techniques, their overall numbers have not grown appreciably, and the public in general have had to do something to help themselves. For example, up to ten years ago many people did not bother to lock the front door of their houses when they went out but this would not be a reasonable thing to do nowadays (particularly in towns). As a result, there has been a large increase in the sale of suitable, substantial locks for front doors. Similarly, the market for intruder alarms, safes, guarding and cash-carrying services has expanded at an explosive rate.

In 1967 a trade association, the British Security Industry Association (BSIA), was established with the aim of promoting and encouraging a high standard of ethics, service and equipment within the industry as a whole. However high-minded its aims, such an organization has to be commercial and inevitably the major companies in the security industry pay the largest contributions to the BSIA and therefore, rightly perhaps, take the major part in running it. The result is that the hundreds of small companies in the security industry regard the BSIA as a 'club' for the big groups who try to dictate policies which will benefit the major operator and squeeze out the small ones.

However, the BSIA does represent about ninety per cent by *volume of turnover* of the British security industry and is therefore an organization with considerable influence. It is undoubtedly the channel to use if any question on major principles should arise. In this case, find out from the BSIA which of the following sections you should approach:

a. Safe and Lock;
b. Alarm Manufacturers;
c. Alarm Systems;
d. Guard and Patrol.

Then find out the names of the Chairman and Secretary of the appropriate section and write to them. Obviously, they will not be too helpful if your problem arises with a company which does not belong to the Association – they will be likely to suggest you use one of their member companies in the future.

It may be of interest to note that the Alarm Systems section creates policies to ensure high standards of screening and training of employees, and codes of practice are issued. The Guard and Patrol section places emphasis on proper insurance-cover of potential liability to their customers and operation of stringent screening for all prospective employees.

When dealing with commercial security the contractual arrangements often cause people concern. As in every business situation it is important to read the contract you are proposing to enter into very carefully, to see what you are and are not getting for your money. This is easy enough to say, but all too often people rush off to get security assistance in the emotional turmoil of having been attacked in some way, and as a result seldom deal with the matter as rationally as they should. The only advice to give is – calm down and deal with the matter logically and sensibly. If, however, you do not wish to analyse what should be done and how, make sure of using a company which belongs to an association through which you have some access if things go wrong.

Your Neighbourhood

The role that people, collectively, can play in helping to achieve security has already been mentioned. One of the most valuable aspects of being part of a community is the mutual help that members can give to each other. This means taking an interest in other people's needs and being prepared to respond to them when they are in difficulties. If you see someone hanging about in your neighbour's front garden, take the trouble to pick up the telephone and ask your neighbour if he knows who it is; or, if there's no reply, ring your local police station and tell them. Far better that the police should come and find no harm was intended than that the house be burgled. Equally, if you see smoke coming from the window of a house, call the fire brigade at once.

Clearly, it is also important that people know the law, so that they understand what they can and cannot do. If, for instance, a passer-by sees a youth stealing an old lady's handbag, he can stop and arrest the youth, but should use the minimum force necessary.

We saw how society set up a police force to help with its security. *You* have given them special powers to look after you – you help pay for them and equip them – so talk to them and find out how they can help you and what assistance you can give to them. The same principle applies to the fire services – have you ever discussed with a fireman how he would deal with a fire in your house? This is surely sensible, given that you would certainly expect help in a time of trouble.

Check List

1. What is the name of your Crime Prevention Officer?
2. Where is your local Fire Station and have you been there?

3. When did you last revalue your house/flat and its contents?
4. What is the name and telephone number of your insurance company?
5. What do you do if you lose something valuable and do you know how to claim the insurance for it?
6. Do you have insurance cover on your possessions when you go away on holiday?
7. Do you know the names and telephone numbers of most of the people who live near you and do they know yours?

Chapter 9
Future Developments

9. Future Developments

A Climate of Honesty

Because security is to some extent within the mind, that is the area in which results can really be achieved in the future. The means by which this can be done will involve using all the techniques, hardware, people and ideas we have been discussing. I mentioned in the first chapter that society had been changing dramatically over the last decade and that the crime statistics showed alarming increases. But most crimes go unreported and often undetected and the effect of, say, doubling the police effort is to increase the number of reported crimes. This in turn will increase the number of prison officers and the amount which has to be spent on prisons.

We talk of 'law and order' and 'crime and punishment' as if each of the two were directly connected – but it is not necessarily the case. We are responsible for the society in which we live and if we wish things to improve in the future then it is up to us individually and collectively to do something about it. There is no point in complaining about the Law being 'an ass' or punishments being too mild or harsh, unless we are prepared to do something about letting our views be known and helping to change things for the better. By helping to build up a climate of honesty around yourself you take a step towards improving the situation as a whole – and remember that the vast majority of people really do prefer to live in that sort of climate.

The next step is to remove the temptations you may be offering to others who may become criminals because of you. You have a real responsibility to protect your property and yourself. This means that you should understand which threats are likely to affect you and then take the trouble to find out what you can do to protect yourself.

This may well sound like preaching, but not all the brilliant security devices, materials and techniques which may be developed in the future are going to be the least help in improving society if the people in it are not prepared to take part in the common task. Leaving things to 'Them' to sort out may be a worse sickness than criminality – at least the number of really 'bad' or 'mad' people is comparatively small and the efforts of the criminologists should be concentrated on them.

There is hope for the future and once this is clearly established we can go on to consider what we need to help us to improve our security and what is likely to be forthcoming in terms of techniques, hardware and people.

Security Analysis

As in all security problems, the starting point should be a consideration of the threat. In which direction can we expect things to go? My own view is that in the future we can expect the following:

- More violent crime, from rioting to kidnap and muggings;
- A higher proportion of burglaries against private houses;
- Reduced police response, with none to automatic alarms;
- Increases in the commercial guarding companies, with probable licensing of these 'private armies' eventually.

This may not appear a very optimistic view – and I just hope that the assessment is wrong – but the facts at present indicate these trends. The increasing frustration of young people and the lack of outlets for their energies all too often cause them to react violently, and this violence will probably involve the destruction of property, arson and an even more prevalent spread of muggings and of attacks on people in their houses. Police effort will naturally be concentrated on this area of crime.

Since commercial establishments have gradually realized the dangers of criminal attack and spent money and effort on protecting themselves (they have also been pressed to do so by their insurance companies), the soft targets have become private dwellings of all sorts, particularly in towns where the chances of getting caught are very slight, and the number of these burglaries is likely to increase.

Eventually, the police will probably refuse to answer automatic calls for help from machines because of the high level of false alarms. The response to alarms will then need to come from a member of the public or a commercial guarding company who will go to the premises and, if they realize an intrusion has taken place, call the police by the '999' emergency service. Both this factor and the increased efforts of the police in handling violent crime are likely to establish a need for more and more commercial guards. These, as well as the rest of the commercial security industry, will probably eventually be licensed. If the United Kingdom government won't take this step, the European Parliament will almost certainly force it on us.

Hardware

As violence increases, the need to strengthen physical defences will become essential and this should be taken into account by architects and planners. The closed-in porchways of many new houses are ideal places in which a villain can hide while he forces the front door; equally, plans of new council buildings should consider the security implications of developing pedestrian precincts which are ideal for muggers in the evenings – and bag-snatchers during the day.

Outside doors and the locks on them may well need to be upgraded, and the use of security film on the inside of windows is likely to become more widespread. The spread of double glazing will also marginally improve the strength of windows, but the proper locking of the windows remains a very important requirement.

Electronics

The application of 'chips' or integrated circuits to security equipment is likely to revolutionize the alarm and surveillance areas of the industry. Sophisticated alarms using this technology will be marketed regularly but while some may genuinely contribute to progress the great majority will be 'gimmicks' which will last for a limited time and then be replaced by the next idea. The proper application of the new devices will require a clear understanding of the use of alarms and the part they play in the function of identifying intruders.

The use of Citizen Band radio for security purposes may well be valuable. Such a communication network could be used to call for help in an emergency, provided that reasonable radio discipline is maintained and someone listening is prepared to respond. Equally, of course, it can be used by criminals for their own purposes of tracking likely 'targets' and giving each other warning of police closing in on them.

Many large commercial premises are already using microprocessors for security purposes. Such installations can provide:

– Access control;
– Intruder alarm information;
– Fire alarm information and response;
– Alarms and controls on services, such as lifts, air conditioning and water heating;
– Logging of the movement of important office files.

Once such equipment spreads to private houses and you have your own computer to control the gas, electricity and log your telephone calls, the same machine will be able to look after your intruder and fire alarms, and possibly recognize your voice at the front door and open it only for you. These ideas are not far-fetched because the equipment to carry them out already exists. Once the application of such systems is widely understood the cost of the equipment will tumble – in the way it has over the last decade for electronic watches and calculators.

The use of video recorders is increasing rapidly, and a visual record of visitors to the front or back doors of a house or flat will be easy to achieve with similar equipment. Being aware that suspicious characters have lurked around your home could be a great help in the face of increasing numbers of burglaries. However, when considering the use of new equipment such as this, it is important to get clear in your mind what you are going to do with all the additional information, otherwise you may be so swamped by it that you end up more confused than before you started.

Legislation

New laws and different penalties are likely to have some effect on security in the future. The deterrent effects of stricter laws and harsher penalties are matters discussed at length by sociologists and criminologists, but are applied in the end by the people through Parliament. Whatever the theories, the effects of such changes are not always easy to identify and as the whole subject is so emotive a wide range of interpretations are put forward to explain the increase in the crime rate.

For the last quarter of a century there has been debate on the subject of licensing individuals or companies in the security industry. At present anyone can set themselves up and give advice, install equipment or provide a security-guard service, whatever their background or experience. In fact, there are cases of convicted burglars setting themselves up as experts in the prevention of burglary on the basis that their experience fitted them well to do so. The Rehabilitation of Offenders Act and the laws on privacy make it very difficult to investigate thoroughly the background of someone who wishes to work in the industry. Such information can be obtained from the police about a person seeking employment as a midwife or county council official, but it is not permissible in the case of a prospective installer of alarm equipment in a house full of valuables.

The arguments against introducing a system of licences have been varied – much of the opposition coming from the police, who recognize what would be involved in operating and enforcing such a system. However, most European countries already operate such a system and the European

Parliament could well insist on our adopting a continental type of licensing, which might not be as satisfactory as introducing one of our own.

Personal Defence

In view of the expected increase in violent crime, it would obviously be a sensible precaution to take lessons in self-defence. This apart, the other points covered in Chapter 5 need only be re-emphasized:

- a. Avoid going to places where trouble can arise;
- b. Be aware of your surroundings so that you do not get surprised – be prepared to talk or scream your way out of trouble;
- c. If you see trouble ahead, avoid it or turn tail and run – there are few medals for victims;
- d. If there really is no escape, then deliberately calm yourself, so that you will be able to think;
- e. Should you be attacked, react with all your strength at the vulnerable points so that you can escape;
- f. Do not look back to see how clever you have been – just keep going to safety.

Finally, remember that if you feel that you and your property are worth defending you have got to do something about it. Don't bank on it not happening to you, but face the problem squarely and decide what steps you should take. Above all, knowledge is the key – know the problem, know where to find the answers and know how to become more secure. Keep safe!

Appendix A
The Police

Crime Prevention Organizations

Home Office Standing Committee on Crime Prevention
  Home Office, F3 Division, Queen Anne's Gate, London s w 1
Home Office Crime Prevention Centre
  Cannock Road, Stafford. Tel: 0785 58217
H.M. Inspector of Constabulary
  Home Office, 50 Queen Anne's Gate, London s w 1. Tel: 01 213 3000
H.M. Inspector of Constabulary (Scotland)
  New St Andrew's House, St James Centre, Edinburgh. Tel: 031 556 4149

At Police Forces
Avon and Somerset, P.O. Box 188, Bridewell Street, Bristol.
  Tel: 0272 22022
Bedfordshire, Woburn Road, Kempston, Beds. Tel: 0234 855222
Cambridgeshire, Hinchingbroke Park, Huntingdon. Tel: 0480 56111
Cheshire, Castle Esplanade, Chester. Tel: 0244 315432
City of London, 26 Old Jewry, London e c 2. Tel: 01 606 8866
Cleveland, Dunning Road, Middlesbrough. Tel: 0642 248184
Cumbria, Carleton Hall, Penrith. Tel: 0768 4411
Derbyshire, Butterley Hall, Ripley, Derby. Tel: 0773 43551
Devon and Cornwall, Middlemoor, Exeter, Devon. Tel: 0392 52101
Dorset, Winfrith, Dorchester, Dorset. Tel: 0929 462727
Durham, Aykley Heads, Durham. Tel: 0385 64929
Dyfed-Powys, Friar's Park, Carmarthen, Dyfed. Tel: 0267 6444
Essex, P.O. Box 2, Springfield, Chelmsford. Tel: 0245 67267
Gloucestershire, Holland House, Lansdown Road, Cheltenham.
  Tel: 0242 21321
Grampian, Queen Street, Aberdeen. Tel: 0224 29933
Greater Manchester, Chester House, Boyer Street, Old Trafford,
  Manchester. Tel: 061 228 1212
Gwent, Croesyceiliog, Cwmbran, Gwent. Tel: 063 33 2011
Hampshire, West Hill, Winchester, Hants. Tel: 0962 68133

Hertfordshire, Stanborough Road, Welwyn Garden City, Herts.
Tel: 070 73 31177
Humberside, Queen's Dock Avenue, Kingston upon Hull. Tel: 0482 26111
Isle of Man, Douglas. Tel: 0624 26222
Kent, Sutton Road, Maidstone, Kent. Tel: 0622 65432
Lancashire, P.O. Box 77, Hutton, near Preston. Tel: 0772 614444
Leicester, 'Ashleigh', 420 London Road, Leicester. Tel: 0533 700911
Lincolnshire, Church Lane, Lincoln. Tel: 0522 29911
Lothian Borders, Fettes Avenue, Edinburgh. Tel: 031 311 3131
Merseyside, P.O. Box 59, Liverpool. Tel: 051 709 6010
Metropolitan, C.P. Dept., 105 Regency Street, London s w 1.
Tel: 01 230 3984
Norfolk, Martineau Lane, Norwich. Tel: 0603 21234
Northamptonshire, Wootton Hall, Northampton. Tel: 0604 63111
Northumbria, Morpeth Road, Ashington, Northumberland.
Tel: 0670 814511
North Wales, Glan-y-don, Colwyn Bay. Tel: 0492 57171
North Yorkshire, Newby Wiske Hall, Northallerton. Tel: 0609 3131
Nottinghamshire, Sherwood Lodge, Arnold, Notts. Tel: 0602 269700
Royal Ulster, 'Brooklyn', Knock Road, Belfast. Tel: 0232 650222
South Wales, Waterton, Bridgend, Mid. Glam. Tel: 0656 55555
South Yorkshire, Snig Hill, Sheffield, S. Yorks. Tel: 0742 78522
Staffordshire, Cannock Road, Stafford. Tel: 0785 57717
Strathclyde, 173 Pitt Street, Glasgow. Tel: 041 204 2626
Suffolk, Martlesham Heath, Ipswich. Tel: 0473 624848
Surrey, Mount Browne, Sandy Lane, Guildford. Tel: 0483 71212
Sussex, Malling House, Lewes. Tel: 079 16 5432
Tayside, P.O. Box 59, West Bell Street, Dundee. Tel: 0382 23200
Thames Valley, Kidlington, Oxford. Tel: 08675 4343
Warwickshire, P.O. Box 4, Leek Wootton, Warwick. Tel: 0926 45431
West Mercia, Hindlip Hall, Worcester. Tel: 0905 27188
West Midlands, P.O. Box 52, Lloyd House, Colmore Circus, Queensway,
Birmingham. Tel: 021 236 5000
West Yorkshire, P.O. Box 9, Laburnum Road, Wakefield.
Tel: 0924 75222
Wiltshire, London Road, Devizes, Wilts. Tel: 0380 2341

Appendix B
The Fire Services

Fire Prevention Organization

Fire Service Inspectorate
  Home Office, 50 Queen Anne's Gate, London s w 1. Tel: 01 213 3000

G.L.C., 8 Albert Embankment, London s E 1. Tel: 01 582 3811
Greater Manchester, 146 Bolton Road, Swinton, Manchester.
  Tel: 061 736 5866
Merseyside, Hatton Gardens, Liverpool. Tel: 051 227 4466
Tyne and Wear, Pilgrim Street, Newcastle upon Tyne. Tel: 0632 21224
West Midlands, Lancaster Circus, Queensway, Birmingham.
  Tel: 021 300 5111
Yorkshire South, Division Street, Sheffield. Tel: 0742 27202
Yorkshire West, Oakroyd Hall, Bradford Road, Birkenshaw, Bradford.
  Tel: 0274 682311

Avon, Temple Back, Bristol. Tel: 0272 22061
Bedfordshire, Southfields Road, Kempston, Beds. Tel: 0234 51081
Royal Berkshire, 103 Dee Road, Tilehurst, Reading. Tel: 0734 583600
Buckinghamshire, Cambridge Street, Aylesbury. Tel: 0296 24666
Cambridgeshire, Hinchingbrooke Cottage, Brampton Road, Huntingdon.
  Tel: 0480 54651
Cheshire, Walmoor House, Dee Banks, Chester. Tel: 0244 22633
Cleveland, Park Road, Middlesbrough, Cleveland. Tel: 042 82 2311
Clwyd, Lleky'r Dryw, 259 Abergele Road, Colwyn Bay. Tel: 0492 33113
Cornwall, County Hall, Station Road, Truro. Tel: 0872 3117
Cumbria, Grecian Villa, Cockermouth. Tel: 0900 822503
Derbyshire, P.O. Box 29, Old Hall, Burton Road, Littleover, Derby.
  Tel: 0773 26221
Devon, Clyst St George, Exeter. Tel: 039 287 3711
Dorset, North Quay, Weymouth. Tel: 030 57 6633
Durham, Framwellgate Moor, Durham. Tel: 0385 3381
Dyfed, Lime Grove, Carmarthen. Tel: 0267 31181
Essex, Rayleigh Close, Rayleigh Road, Hutton, Brentwood.
  Tel: 0277 222531

Mid Glamorgan, Lanelay Hall, Pontyclun, Glam. Tel: 0443 222333
South Glamorgan, Adam Street, Cardiff. Tel: 0222 498602
West Glamorgan, The Mount, Mount Street, Gowerton. Tel: 0792 873737
Gloucestershire, Keynsham Road, Cheltenham. Tel: 0242 512041
Gwent, Malpas Road, Newport, Gwent. Tel: 0633 855 677
Gwynedd, Llanberis Road, Caernarfon. Tel: 0286 3811
Hampshire, Ashburton Court, The Castle, Winchester. Tel: 0962 4411
Hereford and Worcester, Copenhagen Street, Worcester. Tel: 0905 24454
Hertfordshire, Old London Road, Hertford. Tel: 0992 54900
Humberside, Worship Street, Kingston upon Hull. Tel: 0482 29303
Isle of Wight, South Street, Newport. Tel: 0983 525121
Kent, Tovil, Maidstone, Kent. Tel: 0622 54207
Lancashire, Garstang Road, Fulwood, Preston. Tel: 0772 862545
Leicestershire, Anstey Frith, Leicester Road, Glenfield. Tel: 0533 87224
Lincolnshire, South Park Avenue, Lincoln. Tel: 0522 33361
Norfolk, Whitegates, Hethersett, Norwich. Tel: 0603 810351
Northamptonshire, The Mounts, Northampton. Tel: 0604 22411
Northumberland, Loansdean, Morpeth. Tel: 0670 3161
Nottinghamshire, Rolleston Drive, Arnold, Nottingham. Tel: 0602 263204
Oxfordshire, Sterling Road, Kidlington, Oxford. Tel: 08675 4211
Powys, Garth Road, Builth Wells, Powys. Tel: 098 22 3576
Shropshire, St Michael's Street, Shrewsbury. Tel: 0743 53981
Somerset, Hestercombe House, Cheddon Fitzpaine, Taunton.
  Tel: 0823 87222
Staffordshire, Pirehill, Stone, Staffs. Tel: 078 583 3234
Suffolk, Colchester Road, Ipswich. Tel: 0473 75363
Surrey, St David's, 70 Wray Park Road, Reigate. Tel: 073 72 42444
East Sussex, 24 King Henry's Road, Lewes. Tel: 079 16 3333
West Sussex, Northgate, Chichester. Tel: 0243 786211
Warwickshire, Warwick Street, Leamington Spa. Tel: 0926 23231
Wiltshire, Manor House, Potterne, Devizes. Tel: 0380 3601
North Yorkshire, Crosby Road, Northallerton. Tel: 0609 3624
Scotland Central Region, Meiklehill House, Kirkintilloch.
  Tel: 041 776 2341
Dumfries and Galloway, Newall Terrace, Dumfries. Tel: 0387 63921
Grampian, 19 North Anderson Drive, Aberdeen. Tel: 0224 696666
Lothian and Borders, Lamiston Place, Edinburgh. Tel: 031 229 7222
Strathclyde, Bothwell Road, Hamilton, Lanark. Tel: 0698 284200
Tayside Region, Blackness Road, Dundee. Tel: 0382 22222

Northern Ireland, 43 Castle Street, Lisburn. Tel: 084 62 4221

Appendix C
Commercial Security

1. Lock Suppliers and Installers

Aarden Spring & Lock Co. Ltd
Abloy–Locking Devices Ltd
A & D Lock & Key Co. Ltd
G. A. Adey Locksmith
Alarm Call Ltd
E. Aldridge & Son
Alexander & Partner
Alex Wright Alarms Ltd
Armada Security Products Ltd
Armour Lock Services Ltd
Associated Lock Services Ltd
Automatic Safety Lighting Ltd
Banham Patent Locks & Alarms
Barbican Lock & Safe Co. Ltd
Baron Security Group
Bath & Key Security Centre
BCMS Engineering & Exhibitions
  Ltd
J. D. Beardmore & Co. Ltd
F. and F. J. Beesley
Bicknells Southsea Ltd
J. H. Blakey & Sons (Security) Ltd
Bon Automation Ltd
Borer Electronics Ltd
C. R. Bowden (Locksmiths)
L. F. Brenner Ltd
Bridgers, Locksmith & Security
  Specialist Ltd
Brocks Alarms Ltd
J. X. Broderick Ltd
A. Buckenham Locksmiths

J. A. Buckle & Son
Burglary Prevention Installations
Canterbury Security Services Ltd
Cardkey Systems Ltd
P. J. Carroll & Son (Locksmiths)
  Ltd
Castell Locks Ltd
Chanctonbury Locksmiths
Cheshire Alarm Service Ltd
Chubb & Son Lock & Safe Co.
  Ltd
E. A. Clare & Son (Locksmiths)
  Ltd
Clarke Instruments Ltd
Clyde Burglar Alarm Co. Ltd
D. L. Collett & Sons Ltd
Contact Alarms Ltd
Cooper Payne Ltd
Copydex Ltd
The Corner Lock Centre
County Locksmiths (Hants) Ltd
Stephen Cox & Son Ltd
CPW Locksmiths Ltd
Crime Prevention Centre (Bath)
D & D Burglar Alarms Ltd
Dawsons Security Service (Rossen-
  dale)
James Deacon Security Ltd
W. Diver Ltd
Dovetail Securities Lock & Safe Co.
  Ltd

J. Drummond & Sons (Locksmiths) Ltd
W. S. Dyett & Sons Ltd
Dynalarm
Ecolarm Ltd
E L S (Electronic Locking Systems) Ltd
Expo Security Service
Fogarty Lock & Safe Co. Ltd
G. Franchi (Locksmith) Co.
Furnead (Industrial Supplies) Ltd
Geoff Gardiner Security Ltd
GCD Associates Ltd
GKN–Stenman AB (ASSA)
Group Sales
Guard Alarm
Guardian Safe Co. Ltd
Guardian Security Company
Gwenic Ltd
C. Hall & Son (Master Locksmiths) Ltd
H. Harrold & Sons Ltd
B. Hatt (Locksmith)
Haycock & Hogg
Heydale Key Registration Co. Ltd
Homeguard Ltd
Home Security Ltd
Hornet Alarms Ltd
Howfield Security Services
Hunters Lock Service
Island Lock & Safe Co. Ltd
IXP Ltd
JB Architectural Ironmongery
JCM Locksmiths Ltd
Jeffcock Security Ltd
Kent Lock & Safe Co.
Kwick Key & Lock Service and Kwick Alarm Ltd
Labyrinth Ltd
Laidlaw & Thompson Ltd
W. & R. Leggott Ltd

J. W. Levy & Son Ltd
Lister Locks Ltd
Lloyds Locksmiths
The Lock Centre
Locksure Services
Locksmith Services (South Wales)
Lock Systems Ltd
Loksafe Services
London Lock Securities
Lumsden Security
Major Locks Ltd
Mastiff Security Systems Ltd
Midland Safeguard Company
Movalarm Ltd
National Protection Ltd
Wm Nicol & Sons (Ironmongers) Ltd
Northumbria Security Services Ltd
NPL Alarms – National Protection Ltd
Oldham Security Services Co. Ltd
Oxendale's Locksmiths
Oxlox
Penwortham Relay Products
Peter Weare (Locksmiths)
Peter Williams Group
Photo-Scan Ltd
Pickersgill-Kaye Ltd
Pincott & Pincott
Protectall Lock & Safe Co. Ltd
Q Sentry Alarms Ltd
J. Reeder (Lock & Safe) Co. Ltd
Securalert Electronic Sales
Security Guard Company (UK) Ltd
Sentry Alarm Systems
Shield Protection Ltd
SLE (Security Locks & Equipment) Ltd
E. Smith & Co. (Locksmiths) Ltd
Horace Smith

Southeast Security
South London Lock Service Ltd
Speedwell Locksmiths
Stand-Fast Burglar Alarms Co. (Sunningdale) Ltd
Stokes & Sons
Strebor Diecasting Co. Ltd (Locks Division)
Surety Security Services
Sureway Security Ltd
Taunton Key Service
Taylor Lock Co. Ltd
Telequip
P. A. Terry (Security Consultants) Ltd
Texamet Ltd
C. O. Tilney Ltd
Tottenham Lock Co. Ltd
Tower Key Co.
V & A Security Systems Ltd
Leonard Wadsworth & Co. (Security) Ltd
Wales and West Midlands Security Ltd
West End Lock Company
Wickdown Security Ltd
Charles H. Wood (Locks) Ltd
Younger Security Ltd

Chubb Lock and Safe of Ireland Ltd
Stephen Cox & Son Ltd
Dovetail Securities Lock & Safe Co. Ltd
Ellis (Colchester) Ltd
Ellis Security Co. Ltd
Fichet–Bauche (UK) Ltd
Fort-Knox Safe and Security Co.
GCD Associates Ltd
Griffiths Safe Co. Ltd
Guardian Safe Co. Ltd
Homeguard Ltd
New Era Accessories Ltd
Precision Metalcraft Ltd
Rosengrens Ltd
Secure Safes (Coventry) Ltd
Securikey Ltd
Security Lock & Safe Co. Ltd
John Tann Security Ltd
P. A. Terry (Security Consultants) Ltd
P. Thorne & Son (Safes & Security Systems) Ltd
Tower Key Co.
The Welconstruct Co. Ltd
Thomas Withers Security Equipment Ltd

2. Safes and Security Cabinets

Abel Alarm Co. Ltd
Associated Safe Company Ltd
Barbican Lock & Safe Company Ltd
Blakdale–NSE Ltd
Checkmate Devices Ltd
Chubb & Sons Lock & Safe Co. Ltd

3. Grilles and Shutters

Abel Alarm Co. Ltd
Acme Gate & Shutter Co. Ltd
A & D Lock & Key Co. Ltd
Alarm Call Ltd
Aluminium Systems Ltd
Apt Controls Ltd
Associated Security Grilles Ltd
Automatic Revenue Controls (Europa) Ltd

Banham Patent Locks & Alarms
Bath Key & Security Centre
Bolton Gate Co. Ltd
Bostwick Gate & Shutter Co. (UK) Ltd
P. J. Carroll and Son (Locksmiths) Ltd
Cheshire Alarm Service
Chubb & Sons Lock & Safe Co. Ltd
Chubb Lock and Safe of Ireland Ltd
Chubb Security Installations Ltd
Contact Alarms Ltd
Dovetail Securities Lock and Safe Co. Ltd
J. Drummond & Sons (Locksmiths) Ltd
W. S. Dyett & Sons Ltd
Dynalarm Ltd
ELS (Electronic Locking Systems) Ltd
Expo Security Service
Fogarty Lock & Safe Co. Ltd
GCD Associates Ltd
Godwin Warren Engineering Ltd
H. L. Goodman & Son (Bristol) Ltd
Griffiths Safe Co. Ltd
Guardian Safe Co. Ltd
Guardian Security Group
B. Hatt (Locksmith)
Henderson Doors Ltd
Homeguard Ltd
Industrial Doors Ltd
Island Lock & Safe Co. Ltd
IXP Ltd
JCM Locksmiths Ltd
Jeffcock Security Ltd
Killby–Tann
J. W. Levy & Son Ltd

Lingfield Alarm Supplies Co. Ltd
Lloyds Locksmiths
The Lock Centre
Locksmith Services (South Wales)
Lock Systems Ltd
Loksafe Services
Loksure Services
London Lock Securities
Lowland Shutters Ltd
Macwood (London) Ltd
Major Locks Ltd
Mercian Shutters Ltd
Midland Safeguard Company
Oldham Security Services Co. Ltd
Oxendale's Locksmiths
Oxlox
Pincott & Pincott
Plan Partitions Ltd (Security Division)
Pollard of London Ltd
D. W. Price (Enfield) Ltd
Protectall Lock & Safe Co. Ltd
Q Security Alarms Ltd
J. Reeder (Lock & Safe) Co. Ltd
Roller Shutters Ltd
Securalert Electronics (Sales) Ltd
Security Guard Company (UK) Ltd
Sentry Alarm Systems
Shutters Doors Ltd
E. Smith & Co. (Locksmiths) Ltd
Horace Smith
South London Lock Service Ltd
Speedwell Locksmiths
Stand-Fast Burglar Alarm Co. (Sunningdale) Ltd
Stanley Automatic Doors Ltd
J. Starkie Gardner Ltd
Surety Security Services
Sureway Security Ltd
Taylor Lock Co. Ltd

P. A. Terry (Security Consultants) Ltd
Ticket Equipment Ltd
C. O. Tilney Ltd
Tottenham Lock Co. Ltd
Tower Key Co.
Wickdown Security Ltd
Charles H. Wood (Locks) Ltd
Younger Security Ltd

4. Security Glazing

Aluminium Systems Ltd
Alcan Safety Glass Ltd
Associated Security Grilles Limited
Cheshire Alarm Service
Chubb & Sons Lock & Safe Co. Ltd
Chubb Lock and Safe of Ireland Ltd
Chubb Security Installations Ltd
Clark–Eaton Ltd
Contact Alarms Ltd
Elemeta–Security Ltd
ELS (Electronic Locking Systems) Ltd
Guardian Safe Co. Ltd
Howfield Security Services
IXP Ltd
Killby–Tann
Mitra (Plastics) Ltd
Pilkington Brothers Ltd
Plan Partitions Ltd (Security Division)
D. W. Price (Enfield) Ltd
Shepherd, Tobias & Co. Ltd
Stand-Fast Burglar Alarm Co. (Sunningdale) Ltd
J. Starkie Gardner Ltd
Sureway Security Ltd

Triplex Safety Glass Co. Ltd
Younger Security Ltd

5. Intruder Alarm Installers

AB Electrical & Security Co. Ltd
Abel Alarm Co. Ltd
ACES Ltd
Active Alarms Ltd
ADT Security Systems
The Advanced SOS Security Group Ltd
AFA Minerva (EMI) Ltd
Alarm Call Ltd
Alarmco Ltd
Alarm Equipment Suppliers Ltd
Alertal
Alex Wright Alarms Ltd
Alexander & Partners
Alpo Security Ltd
Alson Brook Ltd
Anti Intruder Devices Ltd
Apex Alarms Ltd
Apollo Security Products Ltd
Ardente Ltd
Ariel Burglary and Fire Protection Co. Ltd
Ark Alarms Ltd
ASP Alarm Co.
Associated Alarm Systems
Associated Security Alarms Ltd
Audio Alarms Ltd
Automatic Safety Lighting Ltd
Automation & Security Ltd
Banham Patent Locks & Alarms
Bath Key & Security Centre
David Benn (Security) Ltd
Birmingham Alarm Technicians
Blue Circle (Intruder Protection) Co. Ltd
Charles R. Bowen (Newport) Ltd

Kenneth Bradley Ltd

Bridgers, Locksmith & Security Specialist Ltd

Brocks Alarms Ltd

Brun Alarms Ltd

Burglamaster Alarm Co. Ltd

Burglarm Security Ltd

Burglary Prevention Installations

Burgolarm Ireland Ltd

CQ Alarms Ltd

Cameron Systems Ltd

Canterbury Security Services Ltd

Captor Alarms & Services

P. J. Carroll & Son (Alarms) Ltd

Cheshire Alarm Service

Christie Intruder Alarms Ltd

Chubb Alarms Ltd

Combat Alarms Ltd

Constable's Alarm Company Ltd

Contact Alarms Ltd

Crusader Alarms Ltd

D & D Burglar Alarms Ltd

James Deacon Security Ltd

Don Burglar Alarms

Dovetail Securities Lock & Safe Co.

Dynalarm Ltd

Dyson Security Services Ltd

Ecolarm Ltd

Electrical Fire & Security Systems

Electromatic Security Alarm Systems Ltd

Enright Security Systems Ltd

Excelsior Security Services Ltd

Express Alarm Services Ltd

Five Square Electronics Ltd, T A Alert Security

G A Security Systems

Gardner Security Co. Ltd

GCD Associates Ltd

GEM Security Alarms (Porthcawl)

Gem Alarms Ltd

Gibbs Alarm Systems

Group 4 Total Security Ltd

Guard Alarm

Guardian Alarms Ltd

Guardian Electronic Systems

Guardian Security Company

Gwenic Ltd

Hall & Rhodes Security Ltd

Harley Security Systems Ltd

B. Hatt (Locksmith)

Home & Industrial Protection Services Ltd

Hornet Alarms Ltd

Hornet Alarms (M/C) Ltd

Howfield Security Services

Hoyles (Fire & Security) Ltd

HSS Alarms Ltd

IXP Ltd

Jeffcock Security Ltd

Knightwatch Alarm Systems

Kwick Key & Lock Service and Kwick Alarm Ltd

Labyrinth Ltd

Lander Alarm Co. (Scotland) Ltd

Lingfield Alarm Supplies Co. Ltd

Locksure Services

London Guard Security Systems Ltd

Major Security Systems

Manley Engineering Ltd

Manley Security Systems (Eastern) Ltd

Mastiff Security Systems Ltd

Mather & Platt Alarms Ltd

Mather & Platt Security Ltd

Mather & Price

Max Security Alarms

Maxim Alarms Ltd

Meggitt, Marsh & Co. Ltd

Metropolitan Alarm Systems Ltd

Modern Automatic Alarms Ltd
NCL Alarms Limerick Ltd
NCL Alarms
Northumberland Security Services Ltd
NPL Alarms – National Protection Ltd
Oldham Security Services Co. Ltd
Panda Alarms Ltd
Patrol Alarm System Ltd
Penwortham Relay Products
Phoenix Alarm Systems Ltd
Pincott & Pincott
Pointer Alarms Ltd
PPR Alarm Systems Ltd
Property Guard Ltd
Property Protection (Wales) Ltd
Q Security Alarms Ltd
Rouse Security Service
Safeguard Alarms & Safeguard Electronics Ltd
Safeway Security Ltd
Sarnia Security Systems Ltd
The Scot Security Co.
Securalert Electronics (Sales) Ltd
Securicor Ltd
Securite (Poole) Ltd
Security Alarms (Northern) Ltd
Security Centres (UK) Ltd
Security Guard Company (UK) Ltd
Security Planning Associates (Central) Ltd
Security Planning Associates (UK) Ltd
Security Systems Ltd
Sentry Alarms (Hull)
Sentry Alarm Systems
Shield Protection Ltd
Shorrock Security Systems Ltd
Solar Security Services Ltd

Southward Burglar & Fire Alarms Ltd
Stand-Fast Burglar Alarm Co. (East Anglia) Ltd
Stand-Fast Burglar Alarm Co. (East Kent) Ltd
Stand-Fast Burglar Alarm Co. (Plymouth) Ltd
Stand-Fast Burglar Alarm Co. (South Midlands) Ltd
Stand-Fast Burglar Alarm Co. (Bristol) Ltd
Stand-Fast Burglar Alarm Co. (South London Counties) Ltd
Stand-Fast Burglar Alarm Co. (Sunningdale) Ltd
Stand-Fast Burglar Alarm Co. (Swindon) Ltd
Star Burglar Alarms Ltd
Surety Security Services
Thames Safeguard Ltd
Tower Key Co.
Ultra Security Alarms
V & A Security Systems Ltd
Wales & West Midlands Security Ltd
Warnalarm Ltd
Watson Security
Westronics Ltd
Windsor Alarms Ltd
Y C Security Alarms Ltd
Yorlan (Security Products)

6. Guarding and Patrol

AFA–Minerva (EMI) Ltd
Alsecure Ltd
Anti-Crime Guards Ltd
Armaguard Ltd
Arrow Securities Ltd
Bickenhill Security Services Ltd

Burns International Security Services (U K) Ltd
Centuryan Security Ltd
Chubb Wardens Ltd
Clyde Burglar Alarm Co. Ltd
Consolidated Safeguards Ltd
Expo Security Service
Group 4 Total Security Ltd
Guardian Security Company
Instant Aid Company
Mini Security Ltd
Pegasus Security Ltd
P P R Security Services Ltd
Pritchard Security Services Ltd
Property Guards Ltd
Reliance Security Services Ltd
Rossmore Consultancy Services Ltd
The Royal British Legion Attendants Co. Ltd
Sapphire Investigations Bureau Ltd
Securicor Ltd
Securiplan Ltd
Security Centres (U K) Ltd
Security Guard Company (Cheshire) Ltd
Security Guard Company (U K) Ltd
Sureway Security Ltd

7. Surveillance

Abel Alarms Co.
A D T Security Systems
A F A–Minerva (E M I) Ltd
Alarm Call Ltd
Alex Wright Alarms Ltd
P. W. Allen & Company
Alpo Security Ltd
Argen Information Services Ltd
Associated Entrance Phones Ltd
Bell & Howell A–V Ltd
Bell Systems (Telephone) Ltd
B I C C Limited
Robert Bosch Ltd
Brocks Alarms Ltd
C. W. Cameron Ltd
Cheshire Alarm Service
Chubb Alarms Ltd
Contact Alarms Ltd
Dixons Technical Ltd
Drallim Telecommunications Ltd
Dynalarm Ltd
Ecolarm Ltd
E L S (Electronic Locking Systems) Ltd
E M I Electronics Ltd
E M I Sound & Vision Equipment Ltd
Express Alarm Services Ltd
A. C. Farnell Ltd
Group 4 Total Security Ltd
Guard Alarm
Guardall Products Ltd
Guardian Safe Co. Ltd
Guardian Security Group
Gwenic Ltd
Hall & Rhodes Ltd
Howfield Security Services
In-Store Security Products Ltd
K G M Vidiads Ltd
Labyrinth Ltd
Lakeland Alarms Ltd
3 M United Kingdom Ltd
Marconi Avionics Ltd
Merck and Hollander Ltd
Millbank Electronics Group Ltd
Modern Alarms Ltd
Movalarm Ltd
Phoenix Controls Ltd
Photo-Scan Ltd
Pye Business Communications Ltd

Q Security Alarms Ltd
Reliance Systems Ltd
Rew Audio Visual Co.
RSS Group of Companies
SAS Group of Companies
SAS (R & D Services) Ltd
S & D Security (Equipment) Ltd
Securicor Ltd
Security Centres (UK) Ltd
Security Guard Company (UK) Ltd
Security Planning Associates (Central) Ltd
Shackman Instruments Ltd
Shield Protection Ltd
Stand-Fast Burglar Alarm Co. (Sunningdale) Ltd
Stanmore Video Services Ltd
Sureway Security Ltd
Survey & General Instrument Co. Ltd
John Tann (Scotland) Ltd
Telelock Ltd
Telequip
Television Systems & Research Ltd
T V Eye Ltd
Videoscan Ltd
Volumatic
Peter Williams Group

8. Security Consultants

Abel Alarm Co. Ltd
ADT Security Systems
Alexander & Partner
Alsation Security Services Ltd
Anti-Crime Guards Ltd
Ardente Ltd
Argen Information Services Ltd
Arrow Securities Ltd

Michael A. Ashcroft Associates Ltd
Bickenhill Security Services Ltd
Borer Data System Ltd
Kenneth Bradley & Co.
Burns International Security Services (UK) Ltd
Michael Chapman Security Photographer
Cheshire Alarm Service
Commercial Union Risk Management Ltd
Consolidated Safeguards Ltd
Contact Alarms Ltd
Custodian Keyholding Co. Ltd
Dynalarm Ltd
Ecolarm Ltd
S. Edwards Security Management Consultancy Service
GCD Associates Ltd
Gordon Hasler Associates Ltd
Gower Press Ltd
Group 4 Total Security Ltd
Guard Alarm
Guardian Safe Co. Ltd
Gwenic Ltd
Hall & Rhodes Ltd
H. Harrold & Sons Ltd
Hawk Security Services
Peter A. Heims Ltd
Homeguard Ltd
Howfield Security Services
Integrated Security Services Ltd
Interguard Security Services
IXP Ltd
King's Investigation Bureau Ltd
Labyrinth Ltd
Lodge Service International Ltd
Mastiff Security Systems Ltd
Mint Security Ltd
Paramount Security Services

(Industrial) Ltd
Pegasus Security Ltd
Pritchard Security Services Ltd
Property Guards Ltd
Reeves Security Services Ltd
Reliance Security Services Ltd
Rossmore Consultancy Services Ltd
Sapphire Investigations Bureau Ltd
SAS Group of Companies
SAS (R & D Services) Ltd
S & D Security (Equipment) Ltd

Securicor Ltd
Security Guard Company (Cheshire) Ltd
Security Research (Software Resale) Ltd
Sentry Alarms Systems
Thomas A. Simkins
E. Smith & Co. (Locksmiths) Ltd
Surety Security Services
Sureway Security Ltd
Universal Security Consultants
Volumatic Ltd

Appendix D
Official Organizations

British Insurance Association
Aldermary House, Queen Street, London EC4N 1JU
Tel: 01 248 4477

The British Security Industry Association
68 St James's Street, London SW1A 1PH
Tel: 01 493 6634

British Standards Institute
2 Park Street, London W1A 2BS
Tel: 01 629 9000

The Association of Burglary Insurance Surveyors
P.O. Box 538, Aldermary House, Queen Street, London EC4

Health and Safety Commission
Regina House, 259/269 Old Marylebone Road, London NW1 5RR
Tel: 01 723 1262

Master Locksmiths Association
Sandy Crest, Millfield Lane, Kingswood, Surrey
Tel: 0737 2563

The National Supervisory Council for Intruder Alarms
St Ives House, St Ives Road, Maidenhead, Berks. SL6 1RD
Tel: 0628 37512

The British Fire Protection Systems Association
48A Eden Street, Kingston upon Thames, Surrey KT1 1EE
Tel: 01 549 5855

British Fire Services Association
86 London Road, Leicester LE2 0QR
Tel: 0533 542879

Fire Offices Committee
Aldermary House, Queen Street, London EC4
Tel: 01 248 4477

Index

MORE ABOUT PENGUINS
AND PELICANS

For further information about books available from Penguins please write to Dept EP, Penguin Books Ltd, Harmondsworth, Middlesex UB7 0DA.

In the U.S.A.: For a complete list of books available from Penguins in the United States write to Dept CS, Penguin Books, 625 Madison Avenue, New York, New York 10022.

In Canada: For a complete list of books available from Penguins in Canada write to Penguin Books Canada Ltd, 2801 John Street, Markham, Ontario L3R 1B4.

In Australia: For a complete list of books available from Penguins in Australia write to the Marketing Department, Penguin Books Australia Ltd, P.O. Box 257, Ringwood, Victoria 3134.

In New Zealand: For a complete list of books available from Penguins in New Zealand write to the Marketing Department, Penguin Books (N.Z.) Ltd, P.O. Box 4019, Auckland 10.

Making and Doing at Home in Penguin Handbooks

THE PAUPER'S HOMEMAKING BOOK
Jocasta Innes

This book is directed towards those people who are setting up home in earnest, who have lots of energy and ideas, and – after paying out mortgage or rent – almost no cash.

SIMPLE CLOTHES AND HOW TO MAKE THEM
Kerstin Lokrantz

Some of these garments for men, women and children are traditional; all are functional, extremely easy to make and hardwearing, and the instructions are clear and detailed.

SELF HELP HOUSE REPAIRS MANUAL
Andrew Ingham

Given sufficient practical information, almost anyone can do basic electrical, plumbing, glazing and carpentry repairs. Here is the information.

POTPOURRIS AND OTHER FRAGRANT DELIGHTS
Jacqueline Hériteau

An entertaining guide to the old-fashioned art of preserving the fragrance of herbs, flowers and spices, with over a hundred recipes.

LOUISA CALDER'S CREATIVE CROCHET
Louisa Calder

Cheap and cheerful designs and patterns can make you an expert creator of hats, belts, ties, cushions, gloves and many other crochet items.

Games and Sports in Penguin Handbooks

THE GAME OF CHESS
H. Golombek

'A lucid and logical introduction to the game ... sound instruction all the way through' – *The Times Literary Supplement*

PHOTOGRAPHY
Eric de Maré
Sixth edition

Designed to help and stimulate the amateur photographer, this book gives a straightforward account of the craft of photography in all its aspects.

SAILING
Peter Heaton
Fifth edition

This profusely illustrated handbook caters for the beginner, whether he wants to buy, fit out and sail a yacht or just read the sea-lore and learn the shanties.

THE WALKER'S HANDBOOK
H. D. Westacott

Maps, tents, clothes, Rights of Way, National Parks, the law, shoes, boots, farmers, first aid – all you need to know to walk safely and happily round Britain.

THE PENGUIN BOOK OF SQUASH
Samir Nadim

This is a book for absolute beginners and for people who want to improve their game. Samir Nadim hopes that by following his step-by-step approach more people will play squash, and play it well.